WEATHER FOR SAILING

Also by Ray Sanderson:

Meteorology at Sea

Weather *for* Sailing

Ray Sanderson

STANFORD MARITIME

LONDON

Stanford Maritime Limited
Member Company of the George Philip Group
12–14 Long Acre   London WC2E 9LP
Editor Phoebe Mason

First published in Great Britain 1986
Copyright © Ray M. Sanderson 1986

Set in Apollo 645 11 pt by Tameside Filmsetting Ltd
Printed in Great Britain by G. W. Arrowsmith Ltd, Bristol
Cover photo by G. W. D. Lauder/Pickthall Picture Library

British Library Cataloguing in Publication Data

Sanderson, Ray
    Weather for Sailing.
    1. Meteorology, Maritime
    I. Title
    551.5'0246238   QC994

ISBN 0-540-07311-3

ACKNOWLEDGEMENT
I am grateful to the Director-General of the Meteorological Office
for permission to publish this book

To my mother, who has always been a
source of encouragement and inspiration

INTRODUCTION

This book has been written for crews of small boats, especially sailing yachts. The treatment is confined to a practical account of those aspects of meteorology which are relevant to boats at sea, especially those presenting potentially hazardous conditions.

In this connection, one chapter is devoted to the deteriorating weather events at three well-separated locations as a real, major depression crosses the British Isles, discussing the correct avoiding action at each location. Further afield, another chapter describes tropical revolving storms, giving step-by-step rules for recognizing their approach and for avoiding them.

For those who may wish to take RYA Certificates, this book more than adequately covers the requirements for all levels from Competent Crew to Yachtmaster Ocean.

Ray M. Sanderson

CONTENTS

ILLUSTRATIONS

ONE
Atmospheric Pressure, Depressions and Anticyclones

The wind is simply the atmosphere in motion. Ideally a moderate breeze (Force 4) would make most of us content: much more and the resulting seas become unpleasant and ultimately dangerous; much less and we can't sail at all. That the air moves at any speed is due to the fact that the atmospheric pressure, which is the weight of the atmosphere above a given location, varies from one place to another and also varies at any one place from time to time. These changes are due to the gradual decrease from Equator to Pole in the amount of heat received at the surface of the earth. They are also due to the earth's rotation.

As a consequence of these differences there are areas where the pressure is greater than in neighbouring regions, and others where it is lower. The former are called Anticyclones or 'highs' and the latter are known as Depressions or 'lows'.

In the same way that topographical survey maps indicate differences in height by means of contours (lines connecting all land of equal height), weather maps depict areas of high and low pressure by isobars (lines of equal pressure). Isobars with increasing values enclose areas of high pressure (anticyclones) whereas those with decreasing values enclose depressions, as in Diagram 1.

There is a fundamental difference between these two pressure features. Depressions are areas of bad weather with winds increasing towards the centre, often resulting in gales; anticyclones are areas of good and often 'settled' weather with winds becoming light or calm within their central areas.

Slopes, or gradients, are shown on land survey maps by closely spaced contour lines and near-level regions by little or no contour gradient. In much the same way, the strength of the wind is related to the isobar gradient; where the isobars are close together the winds will be strong and where they are well separated winds will be light or calm.

But here the analogy between land and weather maps breaks down. While water flows nearly directly downhill, crossing the contours almost perpendicularly, the wind does *not* blow directly

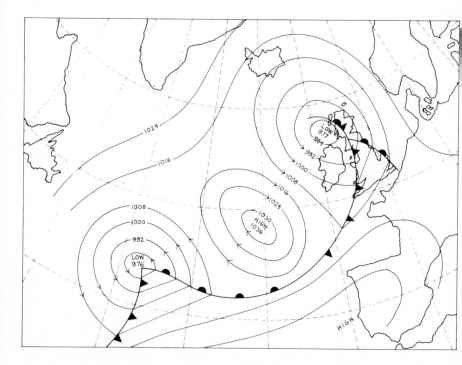

1 A typical weather map showing warm and cold fronts, and
the way isobars indicate pressure differences in a similar manner
to contour lines on maps. A col is a 'saddle' between high-
pressure areas with lower pressure on both sides of it.

out of anticyclones (highs) towards depressions and across the
isobars at a right angle. It attempts to do so under the influence of
the 'pressure gradient force' acting from high to low pressure, but
as soon as it begins to move it is deflected by a force which is due to
the earth's rotation. The deflection proceeds until there is balanced
flow between the two effects: this occurs when the air is moving
parallel to the isobars.

The deflection is always towards the right in the Northern
Hemisphere and to the left in the Southern. Thus the wind blows
counter-clockwise around a low and clockwise around a high in the
Northern, and clockwise around a low but counter-clockwise
around a high in the Southern Hemisphere.

This pattern represents the actual air flow at about 1000 m
altitude, which can sometimes be seen by the movement of low
clouds. However, below this level frictional drag has an increasing

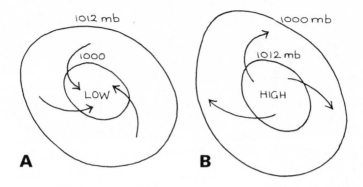

2 Surface winds around depressions and anticyclones in the Northern Hemisphere.

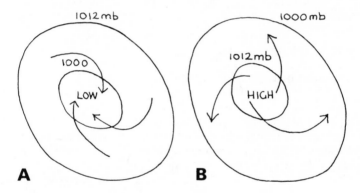

3 Surface winds around depressions and anticyclones in the Southern Hemisphere.

effect as the surface is approached, which not only reduces the wind speed but also changes its direction. This effect backs the surface winds by roughly 30° from the balanced direction in the Northern Hemisphere and veers it by a similar amount in the Southern. (Backing is a counter-clockwise change of wind direction and veering is a clockwise change.) This explains why the surface wind direction is often not the same as that of the wind driving the low-level clouds. The winds felt at ground level around highs and lows are shown in Diagrams 2 and 3.

At the surface, then, there is a minor component of the airflow blowing into a low and out of a high. Of itself, this inflow and outflow would fill a depression and weaken an anticyclone within

11

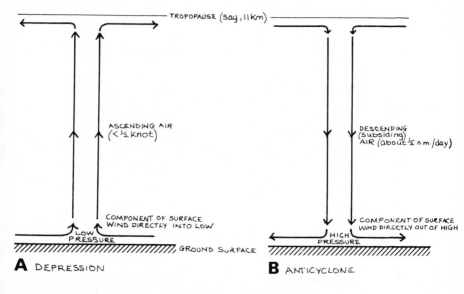

4 Idealized picture of the vertical air movement in a depression and an anticyclone.

a matter of hours. That it does not do so is due to the fact that air also rises within a depression and flows out at the top, whereas it descends within an anticyclone as a result of inflow at the top (shown schematically in Diagram 4). Rising air leads to thick clouds and weather (rain, snow etc); descending air disperses cloud and results in fine settled weather. Vertical airflow accounts for the dramatic weather differences between depressions and anti-cyclones.

TWO
Clouds and their Significance

As it rises air is cooled by expansion, leading to condensation into clouds of the water vapour which is always present in the air. Continuing ascent will then lead to the excess moisture being precipitated out as rain, snow, drizzle or hail etc. Air ascends in four ways:

Orographically — over hills and mountains
Convection — from surface heating
Mass ascent — within depressions and along fronts
Wind shear — due to turbulence at the horizontal boundary between two layers moving in significantly different directions.

Cloud Types
Clouds are divided into three main categories depending on whether the cloud particles are water droplets, ice crystals or a mixture of both.

1. Low clouds are composed of water droplets and are generally confined to the lowest 2,500 m of the atmosphere.
2. High clouds are formed from ice crystals and are to be found, on average, above 5,500 m altitude.
3. Medium level clouds, composed of a mixture of water droplets and ice crystals, are located between 2,500 and 5,500 m.

Some tall columns of cloud (cumulus and cumulonimbus) rise through all three regions but are classified as low clouds since the cloud base is normally below 2,500 m.

As a general rule when observing and identifying clouds, those which appear white, when viewed looking *towards* the sun, are almost certainly high clouds (ice crystal cloud) and those which appear grey contain water droplets; they are either medium level or low clouds. Normally, the darker the greyness the deeper the cloud. All cloud types will appear white when illuminated by direct sunlight, i.e. when the observer's back is towards the unobscured sun.

Cirrus cloud

Cirrostratus

There are three types of **high cloud**:

1. **Cirrus** (Ci)   Wispy, feather-like 'lines' of white cloud often called 'mares' tails'. Invariably the first cloud to be seen on the approach of fronts and depressions, but not always associated with them. Because of their association with fronts, and more especially with depressions, they are, quite correctly, often taken as an indication that winds may increase in a few hours or so.

2. **Cirrostratus** (Cs)   A whitish, milky 'veil', covering whole or part of the sky; it often shows haloes around the sun or moon and is the only cloud to do so. The sun's outline appears rather hazy. Cirrostratus is also an indication of approaching fronts and depressions, but not always.

3. **Cirrocumulus** (Cc)   Small, numerous, white 'lumps' of cloud – an infrequent type and the true 'mackerel sky'. Not of itself associated with any particular weather changes.

Cirrostratus and cirrus are formed by mass ascent. Cirrocumulus and to a lesser extent, sometimes cirrus are formed by turbulence.

At medium levels there are two types of cloud:

1. **Altostratus** (As)   A grey, featureless layer covering the whole or most of the sky. Altostratus is caused by mass ascent and almost

Altostratus

Nimbostratus

Stratus

16

obscures the sun. It is most commonly associated with fronts and is frequently deep enough to produce rain or snow. (The featureless appearance is due to the rain falling from the cloud. At times the rain may evaporate entirely into the drier air below the base of this cloud, which will be at least 2,500 m above ground level and may not reach the ground.)

2. **Altocumulus** (Ac) Greyish-white close-packed 'lumps' of cloud, larger than cirrocumulus, most frequently caused by turbulence. Often called a 'mackerel sky' when viewed in the absence of other (higher) clouds. Not associated with any particular weather changes.

There are five types of **low cloud**:

1. **Nimbostratus** (Ns) A grey, featureless layer completely obscuring the sun; commonly associated with fronts and depressions and from which prolonged rain (or snow) often falls. Nimbostratus is produced by mass ascent. It extends several thousand metres upwards from its base, which may be as low as a few hundred metres, and horizontally for hundreds of miles.

Small Cumulus

Medium-sized Cumulus

Large Cumulus

18

Cumulonimbus

Altocumulus

19

Stratocumulus

2. **Stratus** (St)   A thin, grey, very low layer (typically below 300 m), often very ragged in appearance, sometimes extending over the whole sky. Produced by turbulence or orographic ascent.

3. **Stratocumulus** (Sc)   Sometimes a complete cover of cloud showing 'rippling' due to small undulations in the height of the base; it is commonly formed by turbulence. Stratus and stratocumulus are not indicative of changes in the weather.

4. **Cumulus** (Cu)   Heaped-up cloud formed by convection and sometimes by orographic ascent. When tall columns having a cauliflower shape are present it is a clear indication that the atmosphere is unstable and that showers may be expected. It is in these conditions that the surface wind becomes gusty and more than usually variable in direction (see Chapter 10). The base of cumulus, normally viewed against the sun, appears very dark; when the side of the cloud is in strong sunlight it appears brilliantly white.

5. **Cumulonimbus** (Cb)   A large version of a cumulus cloud, it sometimes extends as a tall column from its base at about 500 m to

Cirrocumulus

2 km

1 km

5   The formation of cumulus clouds. Thermal 'bubbles' first
form at the surface and then rise (1–4); each stage is separated by
only a few minutes. Rising air within the 'bubble' is cooled to
form cloud (5–7). The initial stage (5) is 'fair weather' cumulus.
Later stages (7 and beyond) give showers, thunderstorms and
squalls.

about 9,000 m in high latitudes, and over 18,000 m at the Equator where the width of the column may be 10 miles or more. Cumulonimbus is the most dramatic and destructive of all clouds. Produced by vigorous convection, the up and down currents within this cloud are a hazard to aviation, and we shall see in Chapter 10 that the down-currents produce sudden squalls which are a hazard to yachts. It is the only cloud which produces thunderstorms and hailstones. The base appears very dark indeed and very threatening, often with a hint of purple in its very dark grey colour. Again, when viewed in direct sunlight the side of this cloud will appear brilliantly white and it is then that its characteristic 'anvil' top may be seen. Distant cumulonimbus clouds take on a pale pink tint when illuminated by direct sunlight.

THREE
Air Masses:
Fronts and Depressions

As a result of intense solar heating over the Equatorial regions and considerably less in the Polar areas of our rotating planet, an average distribution of atmospheric pressure emerges as shown in Diagrams 6a and 6b. A belt of high pressure is almost permanently present in each hemisphere, centred in about latitude 30° – the sub-tropical highs. These enclose a zone of lower pressure around the Equator. There are normally further areas of high pressure over the Poles, and low pressure belts between latitudes 50° and 60° in the Temperate Zones in each hemisphere.

These belts of low and high pressure represent the averaged surface pressure at many locations on the globe over a long period of years: they are not continuous. On any one day a series of anticyclones will normally be found near 30° North and South, while a string of depressions may be expected around the globe roughly between latitudes 50° and 60° in both hemispheres. Even this is not an inflexible picture, for the sub-tropical highs may migrate polewards to latitude 45°–55° in summer while deep

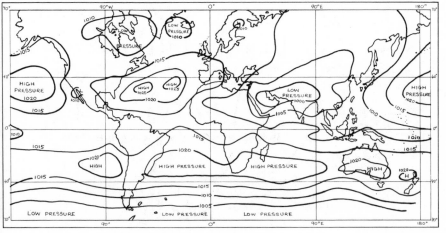

6a   Mean monthly pressure in mb for July.

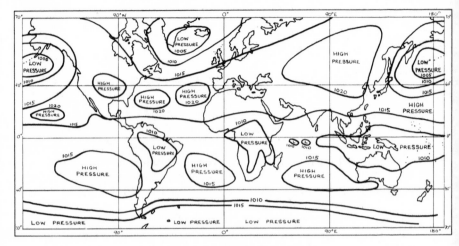

6b Mean monthly pressure in mb for January.

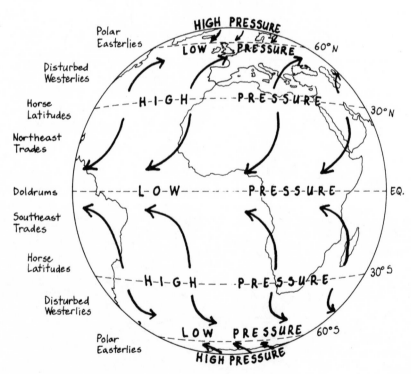

6c Pressure distribution and main wind belts.

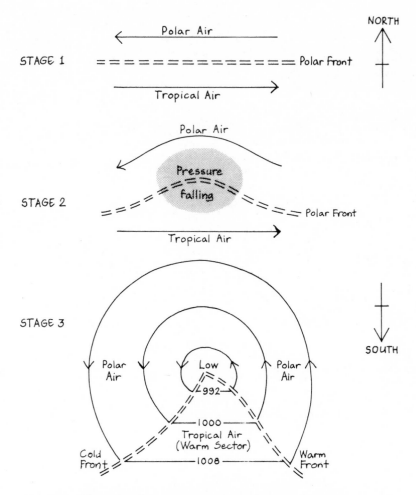

7a Formation of a depression on the Polar Front in the Northern Hemisphere. Stage 3 takes place some 12–24 hours after Stage 1.

depressions may sometimes be found in the sub-tropics, more especially in winter.

As a result of Nature's attempt to reduce pressure differences, air moves from high pressure towards low pressure but is subjected to the deflecting force due to the earth's rotation (see Chapter 1). Consequently there emerges a pattern of mean winds which is shown in Diagram 6c. Air moving Equatorward from the sub-tropical highs is deflected towards the west. These winds are the

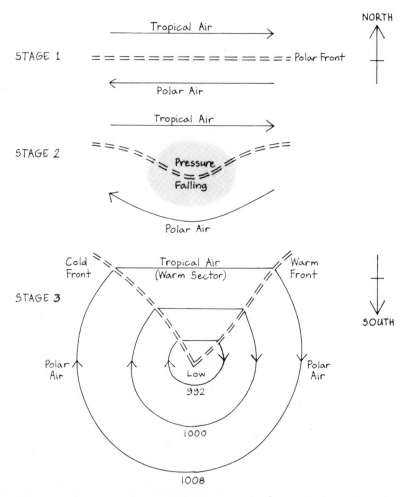

7b Formation of a depression on the Polar Front in the Southern Hemisphere.

Northeast and Southeast Trades: the most persistent wind pattern on the globe. (Note that winds are named by the direction *from* which they blow.) The trades enclose a belt of generally light and variable winds called the Doldrums (though violent squalls may occur with the heavy showers or thunderstorms associated with this belt). Air leaving the Polar highs is also deflected towards the west (the Polar Easterlies), while air leaving the Poleward side of the sub-tropical highs is deflected progressively more eastward to

8a The process of occlusion – Northern Hemisphere.

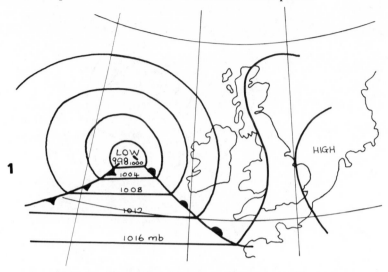

Stage 1: Low moving steadily, at say 20 kt, E and still deepening. The cold front usually moves faster than the warm front.

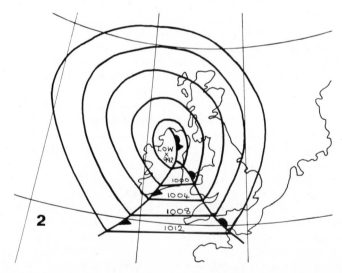

Stage 2, about 6–12 hours later: cold front begins to 'overtake' the warm front near the centre of the low, in the initial stage of occlusion. The low now normally ceases to deepen; it slows down and begins to turn Poleward.

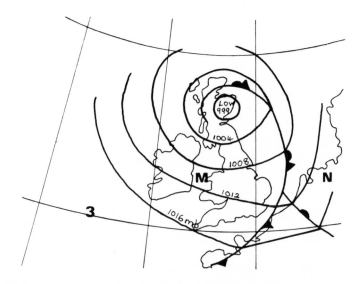

Stage 3, a further 6–12 hours later: the cold front has undercut most of the warm front and occlusion is almost complete. The low begins to fill and becomes very slow-moving, sometimes stationary.

produce the temperate-latitude Westerlies.

Whereas air entering the low pressure belts is subjected to considerable turmoil within depressions, air within an anticyclone is very slow-moving and may remain under its influence for as long as several weeks. During this period the surface air everywhere within the anticyclone will acquire the temperature and humidity characteristics of the home region: warm in the sub-tropical highs and cold in the Polar highs and, in both cases, moist if over the oceans and dry over land. These high pressure belts are the breeding grounds of the major air masses: variously Tropical Maritime, Tropical Continental, Polar Maritime and Polar Continental air masses according to the source region.

Air in the central region of an anticyclone eventually reaches the periphery and then moves out towards areas of lower pressure. The Northeast and Southeast Trades converge towards the Equatorial belt, finally producing the heavy showers or thunderstorms and hurricanes characteristic of this region. Of more importance to most yachtsmen is the convergence of the Westerlies and the Polar Easterlies in about 50° to 60° latitude in each hemisphere. These Tropical and Polar air masses, of quite different density, do not mix as they meet. Instead the warm (Tropical) air, of lower density, rises

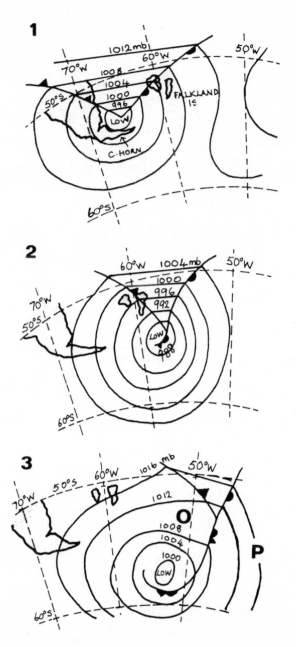

8b Occlusion process in the Southern Hemisphere. For notes, see Diagram 8a.

9 Section view of the formation of a cold occlusion (A,B,C) and a warm occlusion (A,B,D).

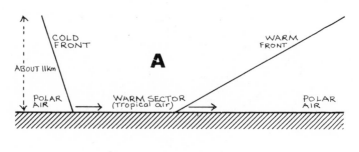

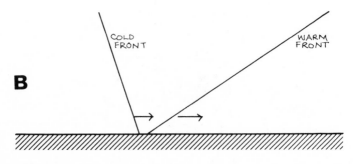

The cold front has almost caught up with the warm front, at ground level.

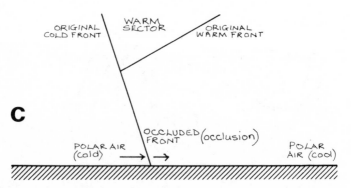

Cold air has reached and moved underneath the warm front, pushing it upwards. Since the overtaking air is colder, it behaves as a cold front and is called a 'cold occlusion'.

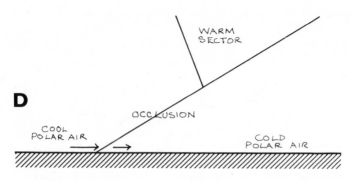

D

WARM SECTOR

OCCLUSION

COOL POLAR AIR

COLD POLAR AIR

Exceptionally, the Polar air ahead of the low is colder than that behind. When the latter catches up the result is then called a 'warm occlusion'.

over the cold (Polar) air at their common sloping boundary which is called the Polar Front. Though this is often shown in diagrams as a continuous line encircling the globe in each hemisphere, in reality it is discontinuous and greatly distorted by depressions. Largely due to friction, waves form on the Polar Front and though many then run away in a general easterly direction without any development, some will undergo a fall of pressure at the wave tip leading to a circulation around the wave (see Diagram 7). It can be seen that the contra-flowing air masses are predisposed towards the appropriate circulation: counter-clockwise in the Northern and clockwise in the Southern Hemisphere. The new depression, steered by upper level winds, will commonly move in an ENE direction carrying its own captured part of the Polar Front, the warm air trapped on the Equatorward side of the low in a segment known as the Warm Sector.

Fronts are labelled according to the temperature of the overtaking air. Due to the direction of rotation around a low, the warm air on the eastern side of the warm sector is overtaking colder air at the Warm Front. On the western side of the warm sector cold air is overtaking (or strictly speaking, undercutting) warm air at the Cold Front. Eventually, since the cold air in the rear of a low is normally moving faster than the air in the warm sector, the cold front catches up and the warm air is lifted off the ground, starting at the central regions of the low and working progressively outwards. The cool air (normally moving from warmer latitudes) ahead of the warm front and the cold air behind the cold front thus form a new boundary called an Occlusion, or Occluded Front (Diagrams 8 and 9).

A new wave may develop on the cold front, typically 1,000 miles

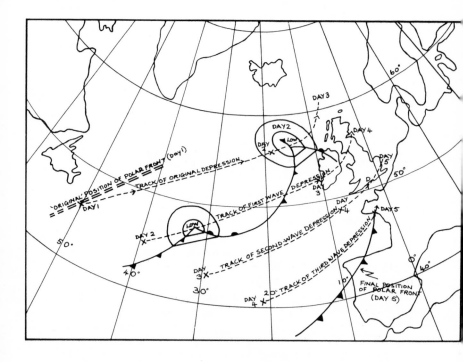

10 Tracks of a train of depressions occurring over several days. They are shown for a time early on Day 2.

or so from the old low, and it will also move ENE. This process may be repeated two or three times, each new low forming nearer the Equator than the last until the cold front, now in sub-tropical latitudes, loses its temperature difference and becomes too weak to generate new depressions. Diagram 10 shows such a train of wave depressions. Shortly after the onset of the occlusion process a depression reaches maturity. It then decelerates, turns on to a more Poleward track and begins to fill.

Another type of depression sometimes forms at the 'triple point' where the occlusion, warm and cold fronts meet. Such secondary or 'breakaway' lows will usually run E or even SE (Diagram 11). Their development is sometimes dramatic, the new low maturing and perhaps absorbing the old one in as little as 12 to 24 hours.

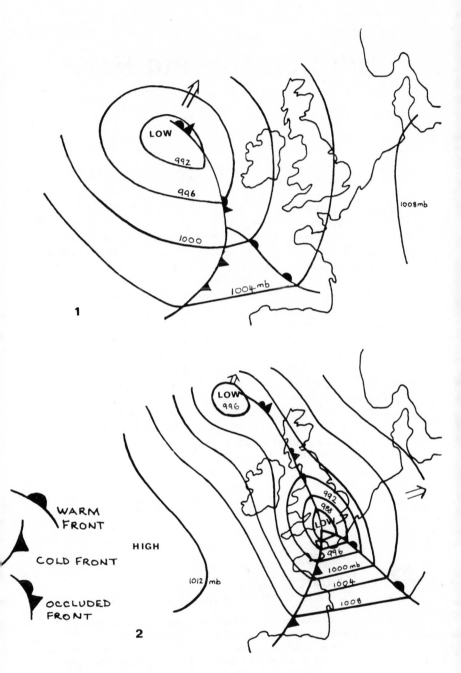

1

2

WARM
FRONT

COLD FRONT

OCCLUDED
FRONT

HIGH

1012 mb

LOW
996

LOW
992
988
LOW
996
1000 mb
1004
1008

LOW
992
996
1000
1004 mb
1008 mb

11   Development of a secondary or 'breakaway' low.

FOUR
Visibility: Fog and Haze

The visibility is a measure of the clarity of the air, which may be reduced by numerous water droplets, or by dust particles raised by wind and convection or generated by industrial smoke. Water droplets may reduce visibility to Mist (1 or 2 km) and to Fog (less than 1,000 m). Haze, caused by dust particles, normally reduces it to less than 10 km and exceptionally to less than 1,000 m; in sandstorms near desert coasts it may be down to a few metres.

In general, poorer visibilities occur when the atmosphere is stable: an inversion of temperature (colder air nearer the ground) is present which inhibits vertical motion and so prevents haze, mist and fog from dispersing (Diagram 12). However, poor visibility does occur when the atmosphere is unstable. Then, due to heavy rain or thunderstorms, it may be reduced temporarily to a few hundred metres. Snow showers will reduce visibility to a few metres, though hopefully this is an academic point for most of us.

Sea fog forms when moist air flows over a colder sea surface. The required conditions are that the dew-point temperature of the air (a measure of its humidity) is equal to, or higher than, the sea surface temperature. In flowing over a colder sea the air cools to its dew-point temperature and fog forms. As a general point, when the

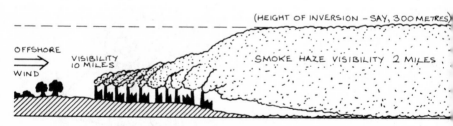

12   Visibility reduced by smoke trapped under an inversion. Temperature normally falls with increasing height, but this change is sometimes reversed in a shallow layer. Such inversions inhibit upward motion and form a 'lid' that stops the upwards dispersal of smoke.

dew-point temperature is $0°$ to $2°C$ above the sea temperature, fog patches covering, say, 20% of the surface will form. Fog banks covering 40–50% may be expected when 2 to 4°C warmer, and extensive fog when dew-point temperature is more than 4°C above the sea surface temperature.

Fog is most common in late spring and early summer, when air (and dew-point) temperatures may be well above the sea temperature. This is especially so in the warm sector of a depression (Tropical Maritime air mass) though it should be expected in most seasons when SW winds range over the waters around the British Isles. Sea fog is less frequent in winter in these waters, when sea surface temperatures are relatively high.

Since sea fog is commonly associated with Tropical Maritime air masses in the warm sector of depressions, it follows that its clearance will be associated with a change of air mass, i.e. with a passage of a cold front or at least a change in wind direction. Unlike land fog, sea fog does not disperse during the day through surface heating.

There is little that can be done to forecast sea fog from a yacht at sea. The best indication by far is constant monitoring of shipping forecasts.

Land fog occurs under different conditions. It requires light winds, clear skies at night and reasonably moist air. Land fog is of little concern except in small estuaries and on coasts. Land fog drifting offshore will normally lift off the surface or disperse within a few hundred metres of the coast, for in winter, when land fogs are more frequent, the sea surface is normally much warmer than the fog clearance temperature. On some occasions fog does persist when it drifts offshore, due to the fog and sea temperatures being nearly equal, but then sea fog would probably already be expected.

Persistent industrial haze commonly reduces the visibility to a few kilometres and on rare occasions to less than 1 km. In British waters this is chiefly associated with easterly winds bringing smoke from industrial regions of continental Europe under a well-marked temperature inversion. In early summer 1984, thick industrial smoke reduced visibility to less than 1 km along most coasts of Southern England in this manner.

FIVE
Winds and Weather
Around a Depression

Strong winds and bad weather are usually associated with depressions. Winds commonly attain gale Force 8 (34 knots) within a low, and in several cases they will reach hurricane Force 12 (at least 64 knots): these are mean speeds and gusts will far exceed them. In the typical pattern (Diagram 13) the winds ahead of a low are backed much further from the isobars than the friction effect described in Chapter 1, while those to the rear are blowing almost parallel to the isobars. Both effects are due to considerable changes in pressure. Falling pressure ahead of a low backs the surface wind – the greater the fall the greater the backing from the isobars

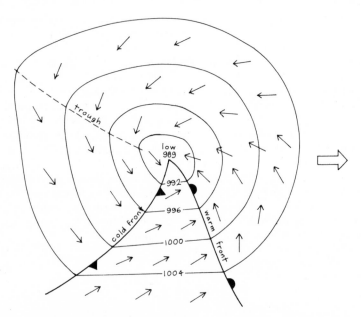

13a Winds at ground level around a depression in the Northern Hemisphere. The direction of movement of the whole feature is shown by the broad arrow.

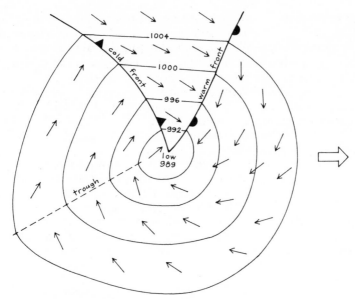

13b Winds at ground level around a depression in the Southern Hemisphere.

(perhaps by up to 90°); rising pressure veers the surface wind towards the isobar direction. In the Southern Hemisphere the effect of pressure fall is to veer the wind away from the isobars ahead of a low and to back it towards them in the rear.

It can also be seen that there is often an abrupt change of direction at fronts: the isobars forming a V-shape which is called a 'trough' of low pressure along the front. These are Frontal Troughs. As the front passes there is often a sharp veer of wind, more especially at a cold front. Troughs are sometimes found in the cold air in the rear of a low, well away from any fronts: they are Nonfrontal Troughs. As these pass there will also be a wind veer in the Northern Hemisphere (backing in the Southern) which can be as dramatic as windshifts associated with cold fronts.

In general, as a depression approaches the wind will back and freshen. (Throughout the following discussion, which refers to the Northern Hemisphere, to convert wind direction changes to the Southern Hemisphere substitute 'backs' for 'veers' and vice versa. Similarly use north, northeast, etc for south, southeast, etc.) If it is to pass on your southern (Equatorward) side the wind will continue to back through NE and N, finally settling down in the NW as the low passes by. If the low passes to the N (the Poleward side), after an initial backing into the SE the wind will veer at the

37

warm front, then veer again at the cold front, now into the W or NW. If the low is to pass overhead the wind will back into the E (the maximum pressure fall is ahead of a low) and remain there until the centre passes by, then it will suddenly change into the NW or N (maximum pressure rise to the rear of the low).

These changes are summarized in Table 1 and are representative of an average depression. The wind veer at a cold front is commonly more marked than at the warm front because the frontal trough is normally more pronounced at the former. Occasionally, however, sharp troughing may occur at a warm front with abrupt windshifts from near E to SW or even W as the front passes.

As a low approaches the wind speed will increase, typically in jumps of 1 or even 2 Beaufort Forces. There is often an increase just ahead of the fronts, though the wind usually remains fairly constant in the warm sector. An increase in the warm sector is a clear indication that the low is still deepening. Squally conditions often accompany the passage of a cold front, with the highest wind

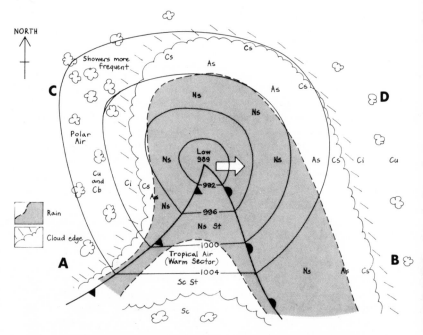

14a   Cloud and weather around a typical depression in the Northern Hemisphere. (Refer also to Diagram 15.) Standard cloud abbreviations are used: Ci – Cirrus, Cs – Cirrostratus, As – Altostratus, Ns – Nimbostratus, Sc – Stratocumulus, St – Stratus, Cu – Cumulus, Cb – Cumulonimbus.

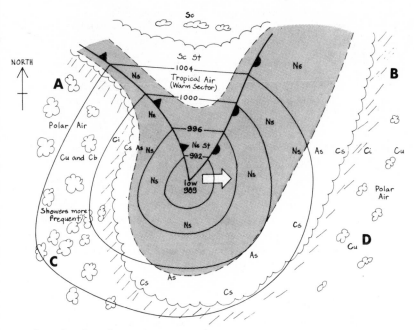

14b Cloud and weather around a typical Southern Hemisphere depression. (Refer to Diagram 15.)

in the squall perhaps doubling the previous mean. Since such a squall is commonly associated with a dramatic wind veer, a yacht should be reefed down even further before the cold front arrives. To the rear of the cold front the winds are usually stronger by 1 or 2 Beaufort Forces than in the warm sector.

Gales typically extend over an area several hundreds of miles from the depression centre. Exceptionally, and chiefly in winter, a vigorous 'dartboard' low with central pressure of about 960 millibars (mb) will extend storm Force 10 (48–55 knots) or even stronger winds for several hundred miles out from its centre, with its gales ranging over the North Atlantic from Iceland to the Azores and from Newfoundland to the sea areas around Britain.

No matter on which side of you a low will pass, the weather and visibility will deteriorate as it approaches. White, wispy cirrus cloud, at up to a thousand miles ahead of the low, will increase and thicken to a grey layer of nimbostratus. Rain, beginning several hundred miles ahead of the centre, will become more persistent and heavier causing moderate or poor visibility, and will finally give way to showers and broken cumulus type cloud with good visibility as the low moves away.

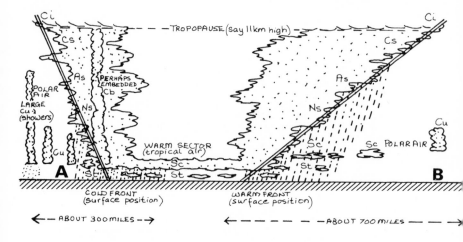

15 Vertical section across warm and cold fronts, shown along line A–B in Diagrams 14a and 14b.

However, if the low passes on your N side (S in the Southern Hemisphere) there is a slightly different sequence of weather. The rain will become heavier until the warm front passes and then will normally give way to drizzle. The visibility will normally deteriorate to become poor at the warm front, and sea fog may well be expected in the warm sector especially in late spring and early summer in the sea areas around the British Isles. At the cold front there is normally a period of perhaps an hour or so of quite heavy rain, sometimes very heavy with hail and thunder, followed by a sudden clearance to showery conditions.

These changes are listed in Table 1 and are discussed in more detail in Chapter 8; Diagrams 14 to 17, by way of cross-sections, show the cloud and rain around a depression.

The above description chiefly concerns the 'typical' depression with some mention of severe cases. Some lows, however, are relatively weak with maximum winds of Force 6 or even less. The associated fronts are often weak, in extreme cases merely a band of cloud with little or no rain and an almost imperceptible wind change as the front passes.

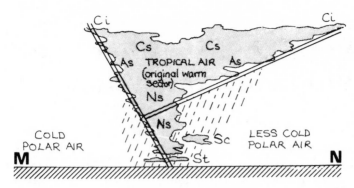

16a   Vertical section showing cloud and weather across a cold occlusion, along line M–N in Diagram 8a.

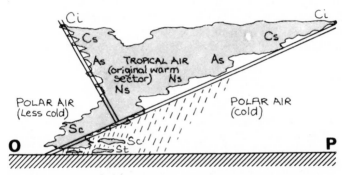

16b   Cloud and weather across a warm occlusion, along O–P in Diagram 8b for the Southern Hemisphere.

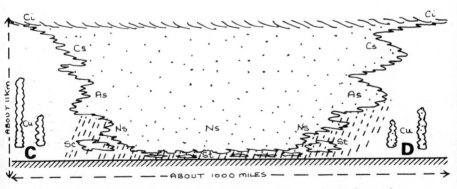

17   Vertical section along C–D in Diagram 14, on the Poleward side of a depression.

SIX
Winds and Weather
Within an Anticyclone

The winds blow clockwise around an anticyclone or high in the Northern Hemisphere and counter-clockwise in the Southern. They decrease steadily towards the centre where there are large areas of light and variable winds which are frustrating to yachtsmen. For this reason the inner regions of a high are to be avoided, especially for ocean passages.

Though Force 6 may be encountered on the periphery of a high, more commonly winds of Force 4 or 5 will prevail over the outer regions, decreasing to Force 3 and less within the system. This is

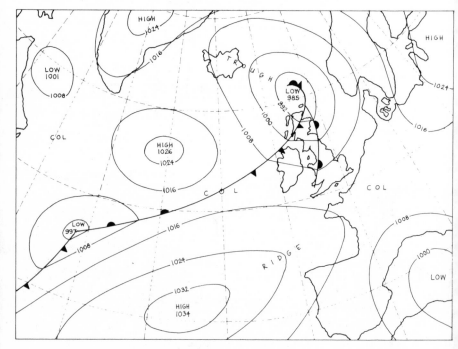

18   A 'windy' high between two lows.

particularly so with the large anticyclones associated with the sub-tropical high pressure belt, such as the Azores, Bermuda or Hawaiian anticyclones. However, some smaller anticyclones, more especially in winter, are much more vigorous. With such 'windy' highs, strong or gale force winds, and more rarely severe gales, range over the outer regions with a reduction to Force 4 or less over a relatively small inner area. These highs are commonly found between two depressions, the whole 'gear-train' travelling briskly towards some easterly point (see Diagram 18 and Chapter 7).

Anticyclones are rarely circular; they are commonly elliptical, the 'extensions' being known as ridges. They sometimes swing slowly around the parent high. If a ridge moves faster than a few knots then the winds on the forward side will be stronger than in the rear and may reach gale strength, more especially when a mobile ridge is following a vigorous depression.

The weather around anticyclones and ridges is normally fair and settled. Cloud layers are thin and often broken and there are usually large areas of almost clear skies towards the centre of a high. Visibility is usually moderate or good. In the Northern Hemisphere the NW quadrant of the high (SW in the Southern Hemisphere) is commonly more cloudy with some light rain or drizzle in the SW winds (NW in the Southern Hemisphere). Visibility in these sectors may fall to poor or even fog.

SEVEN
Movement of Depressions and Anticyclones

Depressions generally move eastward though the track may sometimes be in any direction, even westward. The movement of a developing low is usually parallel to the isobars in its warm sector, that is normally towards the ENE (ESE in the Southern Hemisphere). When occlusion is well developed the low will turn Poleward and decelerate, eventually becoming slow-moving as it decays within a further day or two.

At the developing stage, up to 48 hours, the most common speed of lows is about 25 knots, though individual ones vary widely from this average. Some may move at 5 knots or even less while others may have considerable speed. The 'Fastnet storm' of August 1979 averaged 45 knots for most of its Atlantic crossing from Nova Scotia. A few lows may attain a speed of 60 knots bringing gales into the Southwest Approaches and the western English Channel about 24 hours after leaving Newfoundland.

Frontal troughs swing eastward with the circulation on the S side of the associated low; warm front troughs at an average of about 20 knots and cold front troughs at 25–30 knots, though speeds vary considerably. Cold fronts especially may sometimes move at 50–60 knots. Occlusion normally takes place on the E side of a low and the associated trough usually 'relaxes out' as the isobars tend to become more circular during the decaying stage. Non-frontal troughs, usually on the W side of a low, also swing around a segment of the associated low normally at a slower rate than cold front troughs and rarely survive for more than 24 hours.

The movement of anticyclones is even more variable: they are commonly very sluggish and some may remain almost stationary for days or even weeks. Large anticyclones, typically elliptical in shape, sometimes appear to move a considerable distance. This is due to a local buildup of pressure on one of the ridges and a decrease of pressure over the original centre. This shift of the 'centre of gravity' will completely alter the wind directions in the vast central region, though since the breezes there are usually light it is perhaps an academic point.

Some small anticyclones, escorted by vigorous depressions ahead and astern, will travel at the same speed as the shepherding lows (Diagram 18). These highs, commonly very windy, may move at 20–30 knots or even more.

The movement of ridges of high pressure is not generally analogous to troughs swinging around depressions. Ridges tend to collapse and reform elsewhere depending on the development of areas of low pressure on either or both of their flanks, though some

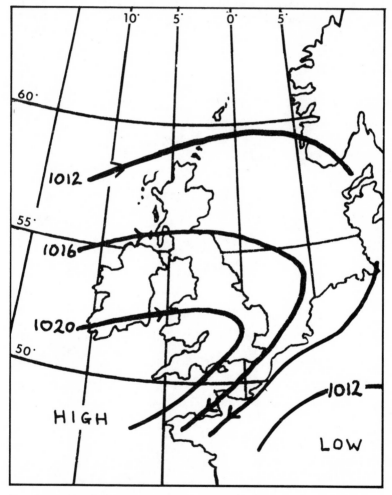

19   Synoptic situation associated with persistently strong NE'ly winds in the S North Sea and E Channel.

swing around the parent high at a rate of about 5 to 10 knots. In summer, a ridge moving SE across Britain from a high to the SW will often become slow-moving for a day or two over central England as strong surface heating maintains lower pressure over France. The NE winds on the forward side of the ridge will then increase to strong or perhaps gale force through the Dover Strait and much of the eastern Channel (Diagram 19). In these circumstances a yacht leaving the Solent with a Force 4 NE will find the winds freshening to Force 5 or 6 by the Nab with a further freshening to Force 7 or even gale Force 8 towards Cherbourg and the Channel Isles. Despite the lee shore, Cherbourg with its sheltering outer breakwaters is then still a safe haven whereas Alderney is not.

EIGHT
Signs of Approaching Bad Weather

Apart from short-lived squalls associated with heavy showers and thunderstorms, hazardous weather is associated with depressions. By far the best indication of the approach of a low is given by shipping and other forecasts broadcast by radio and television or in the daily newspapers. These will normally give 12 to 24 hours' notice and often more. Shipping forecasts should always be listened to before going to sea and monitored during passage. To disregard them will sooner or later lead to unjustifiable risk. The other indicators of approaching bad weather are wind, barometer, swell and the changing appearance of the sky.

If no other means of measuring the wind is available, a good estimate may be obtained from the waves. Since they move downwind they show the wind direction (that is the true wind direction and not the apparent direction felt on the cheek while moving). A good idea of the wind speed may be obtained by comparing the appearance of the sea with the descriptions in Beaufort's Scale (Table 4 on pages 91–2).

A good barometer, reading in millibars (mb), should be fitted in every yacht and this should be calibrated several times each year against sea-level pressures 'now', obtained from a local Weather Centre. (Note that pressure decreases by 1 mb for every 10 m height above the sea surface.) At sea, barometer readings should be recorded in the log every hour. There is then no need to re-set the 'lazy pointer', which after all may have been altered by anyone without the knowledge of the next reader. Tap the glass face gently with the fingers before reading, to minimize lag due to friction. Too much weight should not be given to a change in pressure over only 1 hour, because of internal lag and other possible errors. In meteorological practice the change is measured over the last 3 hours; these more meaningful changes can easily be obtained from the hourly values written in the log.

Clearly a large **fall of pressure** (which must be due to a steep pressure gradient) means that a good blow will soon follow. But how big is large: what is a good blow and how soon? There are no categorical rules, but the following values will give some guidance.

1. A fall of 3 mb in 3 hours is significant and should alert the crew to the fact that stronger winds (perhaps reaching gale force) *may* following during the next 6 to 12 hours or so *if the rate of fall increases.*
2. A fall of 6 mb in 3 hours will probably mean that a gale (Force 8) will result within the next 6 hours. If winds are already strong (Force 6 or so) then even stronger gales will follow.
3. A fall of 9 mb will probably mean that a severe gale (Force 9) will result within 3 hours or so.

Larger falls indicate even stronger winds in a shorter time.

Rises in pressure of these magnitudes will produce similar gales, though a rise of 3 mb in 3 hours will rarely indicate that gales will follow, since the rate of change of pressure is reversed as a low passes by (Table 1). As a general rule, if the rate of rise matches the earlier fall, then the winds in the rear of the low will be at least as strong and probably a little stronger than those ahead of it.

Sky changes are much more difficult to deal with since the range of cloud changes is almost infinitely large. Fortunately most of these are insignificant. At times the sky may appear extremely threatening though no deterioration results, while at others worsening conditions follow when there is little apparent change in the clouds. As a general rule, the darker the shade of grey the heavier the rain to follow since this indicates thick cloud is filtering the sunlight, though this does not necessarily mean a wind increase. However, a more sudden darkening over an hour or less will probably herald a squall; this is discussed in Chapter 10. The sky may also appear a dark grey even in continuing calm and settled, dry conditions. This occurs when large amounts of industrial smoke may be trapped under a cloud layer associated with a low-level temperature inversion (Diagram 12) in an anticyclone. The very light or calm conditions will then allow large accumulations of smoke, producing 'anticyclonic gloom'.

There is nevertheless a pattern of cloud changes associated with the approach of a depression which should become familiar knowledge to all sailors. This pattern, together with the simultaneous changes in the other indicators to give a complete picture, is described in the following account, which concerns the approach of a depression at about 25 knots from the west in the Northern Hemisphere. *Chapters 2 and 5, Diagram 14 and Table 1 together with the photographs may assist in achieving this familiarity.* For the Southern Hemisphere read 'veers' for 'backs' and 'north' for 'south', and vice versa; 'east' and 'west' remain unchanged.

Swell may be the first indication of an approaching depression (see Chapter 13), other than the shipping forecast. When first

NORTHERN HEMISPHERE

Low passing to the N: wind backs to within a point (11°) of SE (and later veers at fronts).

Low passing overhead: wind backs to within a point of E and remains there.

Low passing to the S: wind backs beyond E to NE and N. If shift fairly rapid, then a close pass. If gradual, passes at some distance.

Sequence of Weather with Approach and Passage of Warm and Cold Fronts

	Wind	Barometer	Visibility	Cloud and weather
Approach of warm front	Backs to S or SE and freshens (perhaps to gale force)	Falling, latterly more quickly	Good, becoming moderate to poor	Cirrus Cirrostratus Altostratus Nimbostratus and rain
Passage of warm front	Veers to SW or WSW, and remains steady	*Steadies or falls much less quickly	Moderate to poor	Nimbostratus Low Stratus Heavy rain
Warm sector	Steady SW or WSW'ly wind	Steady or slow fall	Moderate to poor Perhaps sea fog in some seasons	Low Stratus Drizzle (Sea fog?)
Approach of cold front	Perhaps backs a point and freshens a little	Falling	Moderate to poor Perhaps sea fog in some seasons	Nimbostratus and Stratus Rain
Passage of cold front	Sudden veer to NW to N. Squally	Fall suddenly ceases and rapid rise sets in	Rapidly becoming good	Nimbostratus (perhaps Cumulonimbus) Heavy rain Squally
To rear of cold front	Slow decrease in speed and slow backing. Wind is now gusty.	Rising, progressively less quickly	Good, but moderate in showers	Soon breaks to Cumulus and perhaps Cumulonimbus – scattered showers and sunny periods

TABLE 1A   Wind changes indicating the track of a passing depression relative to an observer (Northerm Hemisphere, low moving W to E). The lower table lists wind and weather changes as fronts approach and pass.

*These barometer changes refer to a mature depression: if pressure continues to fall in the warm sector, it is still deepening and stronger winds will follow.

SOUTHERN HEMISPHERE

Low passing to the S:	wind veers to NE and remains there (later backing at fronts).
Low passing overhead:	wind veers to within a point (11°) of E.
Low passing to the N:	wind veers beyond E to SE and later S.

Sequence of Weather with Approach and Passage of Warm and Cold Fronts

	Wind	Barometer	Visibility	Cloud and weather
Approach of warm front	Wind veers to NE and freshens (perhaps to gale force)	Falling, latterly more quickly	Good, becoming moderate to poor	Cirrus Cirrostratus Altostratus Nimbostratus and rain
Passage of warm front	Wind backs to WNW	*Steadies or falls much more slowly	Moderate to poor	Nimbostratus Low Stratus Heavy rain
Warm sector	WNW steady	*Steady or slow fall	Moderate to poor Perhaps sea fog in some areas	Low Stratus Drizzle (Sea fog)
Approach of cold front	Slight veer and slight freshening	Falling	Moderate to poor Perhaps sea fog in some areas	Nimbostratus Low Stratus Rain
Passage of cold front	Backs to SW or SSW. Squally	Fall suddenly ceases and rapid rise sets in	Rapidly becoming good	Nimbostratus (perhaps Cumulonimbus) Heavy rain
To rear of cold front	SW later veering WSW, slow decrease but wind is gusty	Rising, progressively less quickly	Good, but moderate in showers	Soon breaks to Cumulus and perhaps Cumulonimbus – scattered showers and sunny periods

TABLE 1B   Wind changes indicating the track of a passing depression relative to an observer (Southern Hemisphere, low moving W to E). The lower table lists wind and weather changes as fronts approach and pass.

*These barometer changes refer to a mature depression: if pressure continues to fall in the warm sector, it is still deepening and stronger winds will follow.

detected – and this would have to occur in light or moderate winds and small waves since swell is difficult to observe from the deck of a yacht – the low may be 12 to 24 hours away. There is then normally no other sign. If the swell direction remains constant, an increase in the height and a shortening of its wave length (distance from crest to crest) will indicate that the storm is approaching from the same direction as the swell. (A noticeable change in swell direction over 6 hours or so will indicate that the low will pass to one side or the other, probably at a safe distance.)

At this stage, still more than 12 hours from the centre of the depression, wispy, white cirrus cloud or 'mares' tails' will appear in the western sky over a scattering of cumulus clouds, some of which may still be producing showers. In the next hour or two the cirrus cloud will spread over most of the sky, thickening into cirrostratus in the west. This whitish-grey layer may produce a halo around the setting sun and the cumulus cloud will normally retreat towards the eastern horizon. By this time the barometer will have indicated a levelling-out or small fall from an earlier rise of pressure, and the wind will have backed a little and its earlier strength will have gone. These sky, wind, pressure and swell changes are the first visual indicators of the possible approach of a depression.

Although our depression is still about 15 hours distant, the onset of gale force winds may be only 8 to 10 hours away, and so it is clearly time to consider whether the originally intended destination may be reached in time, bearing in mind that the yacht may be headed by strengthening winds and rough seas, or whether to run for shelter in a nearer, accessible harbour. (An anchorage in a bay may not be safe when the wind changes direction as the low passes by.) Further offshore, and well away from shelter, little avoiding action can be taken at this stage since there is insufficient information to determine the depression's track. However, a yacht proceeding towards the W may consider hauling N in an attempt to stay to the N of the low's track, and vice versa if she is bound E. In any case, it is time to stow securely on deck and below, consider what sail may be required, and since the oncoming gale may last for a day or two should the low become slow-moving, whether there is enough sea room, eventually, to run before the wind under bare poles.

During the next few hours cirrostratus cloud will thicken into altostratus, a grey layer of cloud which almost obscures the sun; the wind will back into the S and freshen to about Force 5; and the wind-wave pattern, by now noticeably higher, will become confused and uncomfortable due to the under-running swell. The visibility, though still good, will appear much less to the W than it is to the E and the barometer will indicate a pressure fall of about 3 mb in the last 3 hours: hourly values showing an increasing rate of fall. We shall call this important second stage 'the three millibar threshold'.

In the next hour or so the altostratus cloud will thicken into nimbostratus, a darker grey layer cloud which completely obscures the sun; rain and moderate visibility will soon follow, accompanied by the arrival of a broken layer of low stratus cloud scudding across the sky. The wind will back into the SE with further strengthening to Force 6 or so, and the pressure fall will increase to a rate of about 6mb over the last 3 hours.

The centre of the low is now about 200 miles away (8 hours if at 25 knots), and though it is by now quite clear that a depression is approaching, for those craft too far away to seek shelter it is only from this stage onwards that it is possible to estimate whether the centre will pass to the north, south or overhead. In the remaining 8 hours or so a yacht well offshore can take little avoiding action. However, if she is directly in the low's path and bound to the W it may be possible to make sufficient northward progress in order to remain on the low's N flank and gain the 'benefit' of following gales. Similarly, if bound E, it may be possible to make some attempt to stay in the less hazardous following winds and seas on the S side of the low. In both cases the guidance given below may help towards taking the appropriate action.

If the wind continues to back into the E and the NE, probably increasing to a gale, the centre of the low (unless it recurves) will pass to the S (in the Northern Hemisphere). As the low passes by, the wind will continue to back before settling down in the NW, eventually dropping below gale strength, and the skies will break to cumulus cloud producing squally showers. Visibility will improve markedly and as soon as the centre passes the pressure will rise, at first steeply and then more slowly.

If the sky remains noticeably brighter to the N than it is to the S, the centre will probably pass 200 miles or more away and the winds may not exceed Force 6. If the low is to pass overhead, the changes are similar except for the wind direction which will back to within a point (about 10°) of E and remain there until it changes into the NW or N as the centre passes by.

If the low is to pass to the N then the depression's warm sector will pass overhead (Diagram 14). The SE'ly wind will increase to gale force and then veer into the SW or W as the warm front goes by, remaining steady in the warm sector (unless the low is still deepening in which case the winds will increase even further). Within the warm sector the pressure fall will almost cease (unless the low is still deepening) perhaps showing a further fall as the cold front approaches; the rain will become lighter, giving way to drizzle from the overcast low stratus cloud with poor visibility or perhaps fog, with less strong winds.

If the winds in the warm sector do not exceed Force 6, the centre of the low will probably pass 200 to 300 miles to the N. As the cold front moves through the wind will veer into the W or NW, sometimes very suddenly, and strengthen for a time. The overcast will give way to cumulus cloud and showers with accompanying good visibility and the pressure will rise, sometimes dramatically. In this sector, despite what has already been experienced, a sudden rise, equivalent to a rate of 10 mb in 3 hours, will probably mean storm force 10 or even stronger winds within the hour.

While drying out after all this, keep a weather eye lifted to the W, for the whole punishing cycle may be repeated within a day or two.

By way of an example (and test) of the foregoing guidance, well known to experienced yachtsmen and professional seamen, we shall now examine the indications of the approach of an actual vigorous low which crossed the British Isles during 3–4 March, 1985. This depression brought storm Force 10 winds (mean speed 48–55 knots) across the Southwest Approaches into the Celtic and Irish Seas. For the first part of the discussion we shall exclude the benefit of shipping forecasts.

The track taken by the depression is shown in Diagram 20. Table 2 lists the actual weather observations from the Scillies, Valentia and Belmullet as being indicative of conditions over the open sea to the S, on, and to the N respectively of the storm's track. However, though the Scillies observing station is well exposed, both Valentia and Belmullet are located a few miles inland and are therefore sheltered to a varying extent from practically every direction, especially from the E, and therefore grossly under-read the winds over the open sea particularly at night. Diagram 21 shows the synoptic situation at 0900 on 3 March when the low was at its deepest.

On Saturday 2 March, skies were clearing at the Scillies by early evening as cloud and rain associated with an earlier occlusion moved away NE and a moderate W wind prevailed. By 2000 hours or so cirrus cloud was already spreading in from the SW and would have been visible as the moon was past its first quarter; the wind was backing into the SW and the barometer began to indicate a slight fall of pressure, following an earlier rise. The low was then still developing about 400 miles away to the SW and so no associated swell would have been noticed. However wind, sky and barometer suggested the possible approach of a depression and the prudent yachtsman, realizing that the Scillies offers little shelter from gales, would have considered running for shelter to the S coast of Cornwall.

During the next few hours upper cloud increased and thickened, possibly forming a halo around the setting moon for a time. The 3 mb change in 3 hours threshold was passed at 0200, thus, together with a further backing of the wind and the onset of rain, reinforcing the earlier suspicions of approaching bad weather – though as we shall see later it was then already too late to run for shelter before the winds reached gale force.

The depression's warm front crossed the area at about 0300 on the 3rd, with the wind veering SW Force 5. This veer was the first indication that the low would pass to the N and that the winds, though strengthening, would remain in the SW and later veer W or NW. Pressure continued to fall in the warm sector as the low was still deepening and was still 9 hours or so from its closest approach (see Diagram 20). The cold front passed the Scillies at about 0600

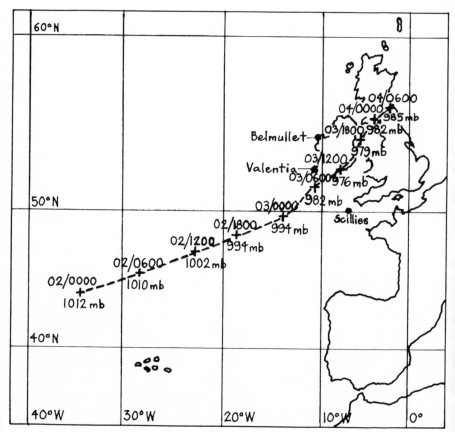

20   The actual track of the depression of 2–4 March, plotted every 6 hours.

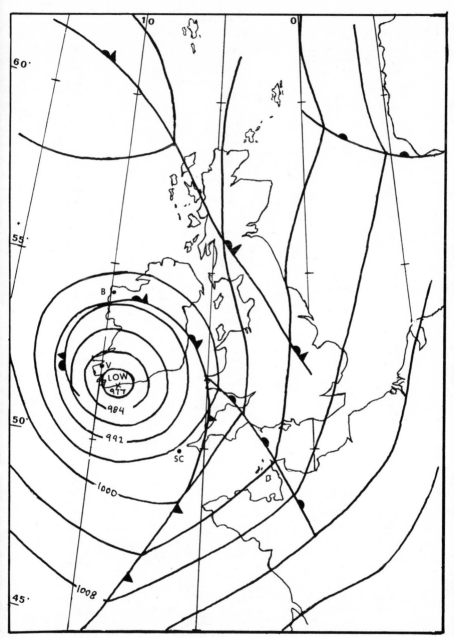

21   Situation at 0900 on March 3, when the low was at its
maximum development.

SCILLIES

Date	Time	Wind	Weather	Visibility	Pressure
02	1800	270 F5	Sl. Rain	Good	1009
	2100	Not Rec'd			
03	0000	230 F4	Sl. Rain	Good	1008
	0300	230 F5	Mod. Rain	Good	1004
	0600	230 F7	Mod. Rain	Good	998.5
	0900	230 F7	Showers	Good	997.0
	1200	230 F8	Showers	Good	996
	1500	250 F9	Showers	Good	
	1800	270 F7	Showrs	Good	998
	2100	Not Rec'd			
04	0000	320 F7	Nil	Good	1003
	0300	270 F6	Showers	Good	1004
	0600	270 F6	Showers	Good	1005
	0900	320 F5	Showers	Good	1007
	1200	320 F4	Showers	Good	1009

VALENTIA

Date	Time	Wind	Weather	Visibility	Pressure
02	1800	250 F2	Nil	Good	1007
	2100	Calm		Good	1006
03	0000	110 F3	Sl. Rain	Good	1002
	0300	070 F5	Hvy Rain	Good	993
	0600	090 F4	Sl. Rain	Moderate	985
	0900	360 F4	Sl. Rain	Good	981
	1200	300 F7	Sl. Rain	Moderate	988
	1500	330 F6	Sl. Rain	Good	993
	1800	340 F5	Sl. Rain	Good	997
	2100	300 F4	Showers	Good	1000
04	0000	300 F4	Showers	Good	1002
	0300	290 F4	Showers	Good	1003
	0600	310 F2	Showers	Good	1005
	0900	300 F3	Showers	Good	1007
	1200	290 F3	Nil	Good	1009

BELMULLET

Date	Time	Wind	Weather	Visibility	Pressure
02	1800	280 F2	Nil	Good	1004.5
	2100	320 F2	Nil	Good	1004
03	0000	Calm	Nil	Good	1003
	1300	070 F2	Nil	Good	1000
	0600	050 F3	Nil	Good	996
	0900	040 F4	Sl. Rain	Good	994
	1200	030 F5	Sl. Rain	Good	993
	1500	010 F5	Sl. Rain	Good	992
	1800	340 F5	Sl. Rain	Good	994
	2100	340 F5	Sl. Rain	Good	995
04	0000	310 F4	Sl. Rain	Good	996
	0300	310 F4	Showers	Good	998
	0600	290 F5	Showers	Good	1000
	0900	290 F4	Nil	Good	1002
	1200	290 F4	Nil	Good	1004

TABLE 2 Observations made at Scillies, Valentia and Belmullet on 2–4 March.

Pressure Change in last 3 hours	Remarks
0.4 mb Falling less quickly	
	3/8 Ci 2100. 8/8 Cs 2300
1.6 mb Falling more quickly	8/8 As 0000–0200 Backed S'ly
3.9 mb Falling more quickly	8/8 Ns
5.5 mb Falling more quickly	
1.5 mb Falling	
0.9 mb Falling	
2.1 mb Rising	
1.4 mb Rising	
0.8 mb Rising	
1.4 mb Rising	
2.0 mb Rising	
2.0 mb Rising	

0.3 mb Now Rising	8/8 Cs (3/8 Ci 1600)
1.9 mb Falling	(8/8 As 2200)
3.8 mb Falling	8/8 Ns
8.8 mb Falling more quickly	
8.3 mb Falling more quickly	
3.9 mb Falling then Steady	
7.2 mb Rising	Gusts 46 kt
5.2 mb Rising	Gusts 43–48 kt
4.0 mb Rising	Gusts 40 kt. 1900 Broken to Cu
2.6 mb Rising	
1.6 mb Rising	
1.4 mb Rising	
1.6 mb Rising	
2.1 mb Rising	
2.1 mb Rising	

0.0 Now Rising	2/8 Ci
0.3 mb Now Falling	5/8 Ci Cs
1.5 mb Falling	8/8 Cs
2.9 mb Falling	8/8 As
3.5 mb Falling	8/8 As
2.1 mb Falling	1100 Gusts 28 kt
1.4 mb Falling less quickly	1400 Gusts 34 kt
0.9 mb Falling	Gusts 35 kt. 1600 Gusts 42 kt
1.9 mb Now Rising	Gusts 42 kt
1.3 mb Now Rising	Gusts 30 kt
1.5 mb Rising	0100 Cleared to broken Cu
1.8 mb Rising	
1.8 mb Rising	
1.9 mb Rising	
2.1 mb Rising	

with the skies clearing to broken cumulus cloud producing showers, though the wind direction remained in the SW as the low was still 6 hours away from its closest approach.

Table 2 indicates that winds reached gale Force 8 shortly after 0900 and increased to severe gale Force 9 at times until 1800 as the direction veered slowly into the W, by which time the depression was approaching the Isle of Man. Since observations from the Scillies were only made at 3-hourly intervals and since ship observations in sea area Fastnet sometimes reached 50 knots, it is possible that the winds around the Scillies actually reached storm Force 10 (48–55 knots) at times between 0900 and 1500 hours on the 3rd.

However, a yacht leaving the Scillies at about 2000 hours on the 2nd, when the first indications of the depression's approach appeared, would still probably have had to contend with some strong or gale force winds because of the distance to run. At an average speed of about 5 knots it would take about 8 hours to reach Penzance, but the inner harbour would not be available after 0100 hours on the 3rd because of a falling tide. In any case, at 2000 there was still no indication as to which side the low would pass; if it passed to the S then Mounts Bay would be a dangerous lee shore for a time, thus ruling out Newlyn and Penzance harbours. Better by far to lay off a course for Falmouth Bay S of the Wolf Rock and well S of the Lizard Race. Because of the extra time involved, perhaps another 6 hours or so and latterly against a foul tide, gales might be expected for the later stages of the passage, but eventually a safe harbour would be reached in daylight.

A departure delayed until 0200 on the 3rd, when the storm's approach was confirmed by further weather developments, would have meant exposing the yacht to Force 8 and later Force 9 winds for a much longer period, though it would soon become apparent, when the wind veered at the warm front (0300), that the low would pass to the N and that the wind direction, at least, would remain fair for Falmouth or, in fact, an anchorage in Mounts Bay which would now offer reasonable shelter. The only other alternative would have been to stand out SW from the Scillies to gain sea room so as to ride out the storm at sea. But this would require a well-found yacht and strong crew and even then might prove disastrous, as the Fastnet Storm of August 1979 unforgettably demonstrated.

Nevertheless, the indicators described earlier in this chapter provided good notice of the approaching storm when first seen,

Satellite picture of the depression of 3 March at 0900 when it was off SW Ireland.

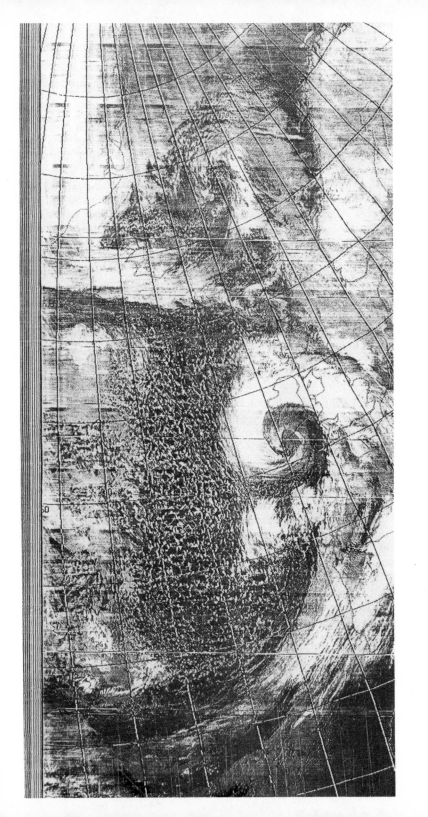

though the 3 mb threshold provided barely adequate notice when the safe haven was many hours away.

All of this has assumed that the shipping forecasts had not been heard, as might have happened either because of equipment failure or even, perhaps, indifference. At the beginning of this chapter it was claimed that shipping forecasts are the earliest and best indicators, of approaching bad weather. Table 3 shows that the depression was first mentioned in the 0555 broadcast on Saturday 2 March. At that time the 'low' was a minor wave on a cold front some 300 miles or so N of the Azores. The deepening low was forecast to move rather quickly (at 25–35 knots) NE to West Sole by midnight that night. Clearly this would present a serious hazard to small craft near the Scillies during the following day. By extrapolating its movement at 30 knots towards the NE, this low might be expected near Dublin by midday on Sunday, 3 March. An error of only $5°$ to $10°$ in direction of its forecast track would bring it over the Bristol Channel at that time, however. In either case, gales could be expected over the W Channel and the Irish and Celtic Seas before daybreak on Sunday. Due to the limited opening times of the tidal dock gates at Penzance, and the chance of strong SE'ly winds by the time of arrival in Mount's Bay, the Falmouth Bay area would be the best option for a safe harbour that could be entered at any time. Since the passage might take 12 to 15 hours, an early departure would be preferable so as to cover most of the passage in daylight and to arrive in good time in case the low moved faster than expected. After all, if we calculate on 35 knots (the upper end of the 'rather quickly' range of movement), then gales would be expected over the area before midnight! From the 'midday' forecast, the low was expected in Sole 998 mb, and still moving rather quickly NE. Extrapolation at 30 knots places it well into Fastnet by midday on Sunday, threatening gales over SW England shortly before daybreak and confirming the wisdom of leaving the Scillies early.

The forecast broadcast at 1750 on Saturday the 2nd placed the low in Lundy by midday on Sunday, deepened to 978 mb and threatening storm Force 10 winds in sea area Plymouth by that time, with Force 8 gales to arrive soon after midnight. The crew arriving in Falmouth Bay at this time would be justifiably pleased with their decision to leave the Scillies about 12 hours earlier.

The next shipping forecast, at midnight on Saturday, put the low over SW England and 978 mb by 1800 Sunday, with forecast winds in Plymouth rising from Force 7 to gale Force 8 and perhaps storm Force 10 later.

This real example clearly demonstrates the need to listen to all

Time of broadcast	Time of gen. synopsis	General synopsis and Forecast
Sat 2nd 0555	Sat 2nd 0000	Developing low moving rather quickly NE, expected W Sole 998 by midnight tonight. **Forecast**: gales threatened later in Biscay and Finisterre. Winds becoming Force 7 in the Channel.
Sat 2nd 1355	Sat 2nd 0600	Developing low moving rather quickly E, expected Sole 998 by 0600 tomorrow. **Forecast**: winds increasing to Force 8 in W Channel and to Force 9 in Sole and Finisterre.
Sat 2nd 1750	Sat 2nd 1200	Deepening low 500 miles SW of Ireland 1000, expected Lundy 987 by 1200 tomorrow. **Forecast**: winds increasing to Force 8 in Celtic Sea and W Channel and to storm Force 10 in Plymouth, Fastnet and Sole.
Sun 3rd 0033	Sun 3rd 1800	Low 100 miles W of Sole 994, expected SW England 978 by 1800 Sunday. **Forecast**: increasing to storm Force 10 in Channel and Celtic Sea and to Force 8 in Irish Sea.
Sun 3rd 0555	Sun 3rd 0000	Low NW Sole 987, expected Humber 985 by midnight tonight. **Forecast**: storm Force 10 in W Channel and Celtic Sea. Force 8 gales most other areas around UK.
Sun 3rd 1355	Sun 3rd 0600	Low SW Ireland 982, expected NE England 977 by 0600 tomorrow. **Forecast**: storm Force 10 in Channel and Celtic and Irish Seas. Gale Force 8 elsewhere.
Sun 3rd 1750	Sun 3rd 1200	Low S Ireland 976, expected Forth 985 by 1200 tomorrow. **Forecast**: storm Force 10 in Channel and Celtic and Irish Seas. Gale Force 8 elsewhere.

TABLE 3   General synopses and forecasts, from actual Shipping Forecasts broadcast on 2–3 March.

shipping forecasts, especially when sailing in vulnerable areas, and to act in good time by calculating ahead from the information given in the general synopsis. The wise decision to leave the Scillies shortly after the 0555 forecast on Saturday the 2nd, which gave about 24 hours' notice of the onset of gales in sea area Plymouth, would have meant a safe passage to Falmouth with W or SW winds of only Force 4 or 5 increasing to Force 6 (as was correctly forecast at that time) and an arrival soon after dusk.

Assuming our 'indifferent' crew interpreted the first indications of the approaching low correctly and left at about 2000 on Saturday evening, and was able to navigate clear of the Scillies in the dark, they would still have had to deal with gales for the latter part of the trip. If, as is more likely, the decision was delayed until '3 mb in 3 hours' confirmation was experienced, then the yacht would have had to contend with gales rising to storm Force 10 at times for much of the passage, placing yacht, crew and rescue services at unjustifiable risk. A 'let's leave it till daybreak' attitude would probably have meant the loss of the yacht.

The wind changes at Valentia, lying on the storm's track, were more rapid and more dramatic (see Table 2). The first signs appeared at 1600 on the 2nd and were reinforced at 2200 by the 3 mb rule and also by further backing of the surface wind and thickening of the upper cloud. Valentia enjoys considerable sheltering in E'ly winds, and especially at night as it is inland. At sea the winds would probably have been at least 2 or 3 Beaufort Forces higher. By midnight the wind had backed into the E and stayed close to that direction, indicating that the low would pass almost overhead (see Table 1). It can be seen that the pressure fall had steepened to about 9 mb in 3 hours by 0300 on Sunday, warning of Force 9 or stronger winds to come. At 0900 the barometer indicated that the pressure had stopped falling and the wind suddenly changed to N'ly as the centre of the low passed within a few miles. The mainly NW winds thereafter, gusting to nearly 50 knots at times, probably reached mean speeds of Force 9 or 10 over the open sea. The rate of rise of pressure at Valentia after the storm had passed was considerable (more than 7 mb in 3 hours) at 1200 on Sunday the 3rd; this was compatible with the violent winds which then prevailed at sea.

Since gales probably set in around Valentia at about 0400 hours, the 'first indicators' gave about 12 hours' notice and the 3 mb rule gave about 6 hours' notice of the onset of Force 8 winds. A yacht sailing only 10 to 15 miles offshore might well have needed most of this 6 hour period to beat back against strengthening E'ly winds and rising seas.

At Belmullet, where the low passed to the S, the changes took place more slowly, as shown in Table 2. The first signs appeared at about 2100 on the 2nd though they were not confirmed by the 3 mb threshold till 0300. Again, Belmullet is sheltered, especially from the E and NE. Winds at sea by 0300 may well have backed to ENE Force 5 and it is estimated that gales set in from the NE by 1000. The Table shows a steady backing through N as the centre passed to the S, with gusts later exceeding 40 knots which probably equated to Force 9 winds offshore during the afternoon.

In all three cases the first signs of the approach of the low (cirrus increasing from the W accompanied by the wind backing and the beginnings of a pressure fall) appeared 10 to 12 hours before the onset of the associated gales. These indications were supported by the 3 mb in 3 hours threshold with accompanying further backing and freshening of the wind and thickening upper cloud, about 4 to 6 hours before Force 8 winds arrived. Further, Table 2 clearly confirms the guidance predicting the depression's track relative to our yacht.

At Valentia the wind backed into the E and stayed close to that direction while pressure fell dramatically, before the direction suddenly changed to N as the centre of the low passed close by (see Diagram 21). At the Scillies, having backed into the SE the wind veered into the SW, indicating that the depression would pass to the N; while at Belmullet the direction backed steadily through N into the NW as the low passed to the S.

Though there are occasions when the first signs of an approaching low are not followed by any real deterioration, and even with a fall rate of 3 mb in 3 hours the subsequent winds sometimes don't exceed Force 5, sailors in vulnerable areas such as the Scillies should keep a weather eye lifted for the first signs of an approaching low as well as monitoring all shipping forecasts. If sailing in less exposed areas where an accessible and safe harbour may be reached within a few hours, the decision to seek shelter may be left till the 3 mb stage, though getting there may require the full 4 to 6 hours' notice if it means a hard beat against a spring tide.

Beware of anchorages in bays and the like which, though offering good shelter from the present wind direction, may become dangerous when the wind changes as the low passes. If forced to seek shelter in an anchorage, choose one after it has been decided on which side the low will pass (Table 1) and in any case have an alternative in hand just in case! If there is no safe harbour or anchorage within striking distance then stand out into the open sea in a direction determined by the storm's track, in order to gain sea room, and then heave-to under bare poles or run before the wind as conditions dictate. In the particular example discussed above, a course southwards from the Scillies would be best, with sea room to subsequently run up-Channel if necessary; or if the low was to pass over or S of the Scillies, then a W'ly course out into sea area Fastnet would provide plenty of sea room to run before the depression's 'NE' winds.

NINE
Signs of Approaching Good Weather

As described in Chapters 3 and 8, one depression with its associated gales and very rough seas may be followed by another within a period of 24 hours or so and the interval of quieter weather may last only for a few hours. To distinguish between this temporary improvement and a more settled spell lasting 2 or 3 days or more, the indications described in the previous chapter also apply. If they again occur a further depression is on its way.

However, after a depression has passed by, a steady moderation of the strong or gale northwesterlies accompanied by a steady rise of pressure, say 3 mb in 3 hours following an initial sharper rise, are the first indications of a possible settled spell. If this is to be realized wind and seas will continue to moderate, and there will be an absence of any significant or increasing underlying swell. Cumulus cloud will decrease in depth, showers will die out and the barometer will show a continuing though reduced pressure rise. Wisps of cirrus cloud may appear on the western horizon but they will not indicate any deterioration unless they thicken in the sequence described in the previous chapters.

These signs indicate that an area of high pressure, an anticyclone or a ridge, is gradually extending over your area. If the spell of settled weather is to continue, these changes will be maintained in much the same manner. The NW wind will continue to moderate to say Force 3 or 4, perhaps backing into the W but no farther; seas will continue to decrease and there will be no significant underlying swell. (In the open sea there is nearly always some swell, even in settled conditions: should this increase and become more noticeable the settled spell is unlikely to continue.) The barometer will indicate a continuing small pressure rise and cumulus cloud will remain small, perhaps levelling out into a broken layer of stratocumulus. At this stage, typically 12 to 24 hours after the low has passed, the good weather will probably last for another 24 hours or possibly much more. In fact it will continue until such time as high cloud increases and thickens from the W and the wind begins to back and freshen, accompanied by a fall of pressure.

The slowly approaching anticyclone may be a very large feature especially in summer and this may become slow-moving in your area for days or even weeks. The central pressure of such an anticyclone may approach 1040 mb, perhaps a little higher in winter, though the average is a little over 1030. (Highs over the continents in winter may exceed 1060.) As a low moves away and the pressure rises steadily past 1013 mb (the global average) towards 1020 a few days of 'quiet' weather may be expected. If pressure continues to rise slowly towards 1030 mb then a few days of quiet weather may be expected with greater certainty. On the other hand, if the pressure rise is much greater, say 3 to 4 mb in 3 hours or it rises from about 1015 to 1030 mb then the high is probably of the more mobile, 'windy' type (described in Chapter 6) and the first indications of approaching bad weather may be expected within the next 12 to 24 hours.

Apart from shipping forecasts, there is little to indicate the further movements of a large, slow-moving anticyclone with its vast area of light and variable winds which are commonly insufficient to drive a yacht. Since these highs are normally elliptical, with the long axis usually lying E to W, or more particularly ENE to WSW, a yacht on ocean passage in the Northern Hemisphere should attempt to haul northwards if bound to the E, and southwards if bound W, in order to pick up favourable winds.

TEN
Winds
Variability, Coastal Effects, Sea and Land Breezes

Even a very brief experience of the wind will soon reveal its chief characteristic, its variability. It changes direction and speed from place to place and from time to time. This is as true in the short term of less than a minute or so as it is over longer periods, from day to day or, in some parts of the world, from season to season. The main reason for the short-term variability is turbulence induced by the roughness of the surface over which the wind is blowing: the rougher the ground, trees, buildings, small hills, etc the greater the variability. However, even along a low-lying coast onshore winds will still be seen to have a degree of variability of both direction and speed.

The amount of variability depends on the wind speed and the stability of the air. It increases with increasing wind speed and is

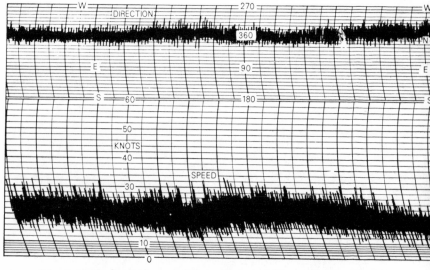

22   A typical wind record (anemogram). Two simultaneous tracings give wind direction in 0–360° (above) and speed in knots (below). The vertical curves represent 15 minute intervals.

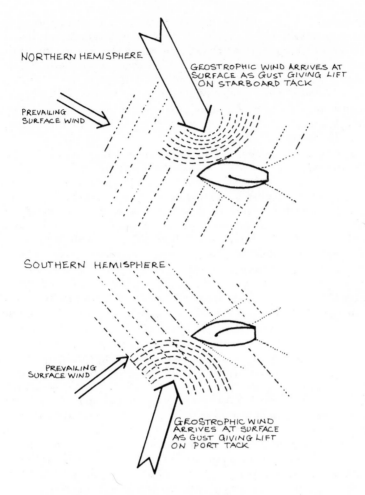

23 Wind shifts caused by gusts. The wind veers in gusts in the Northern Hemisphere, and backs in the Southern.

also much more when the air is unstable, i.e. convection is uninhibited and cumulus clouds develop, than when it is stable with little or no vertical motion from the surface. Diagram 22 shows a wind trace (anemogram) typical of conditions over the sea. It can be seen that even in the 'steady' conditions shown, the wind direction frequently swings 15% or so either side of the mean, and that the wind speed also varies, often by about 15% and less frequently by about 40° from the mean. The gusts (peaks) tend to coincide with short-term veering and the lulls with backing.

Moreover, there is a fairly regular periodicity in these short-term variations with veer following veer every 5 to 10 minutes, though the larger changes are more random. Since the total swing in this period is about 40° a knowledge of this pattern has obvious advantages when racing, especially on windward legs. Whether racing or not, it is because of this continual shifting that a good helmsman will keep pointing up when beating to windward, though an even more efficient method is to steer to telltales flying from the headsail luff.

The effect of friction in backing the wind at ground level from the direction at about 1 km above (veering in the Southern Hemisphere) is described in Chapter 1. The change in direction over different heights is called wind 'shear'. When the atmosphere is very stable there is noticeable shear between deck and masthead, with the wind direction at the masthead being veered from that at deck level. Tell-tales on the leech of the main will indicate the amount of this shear and the mainsheet and kicking strap (boom vang) should be adjusted to make the tell-tales fly true.

Friction not only backs the surface wind, it also reduces its speed. The stronger gusts are the higher level wind briefly beating down on the surface as turbulence transfers energy. This higher level air retains its direction and speed as it descends to the ground, where it arrives as a gust (Diagram 23). All other things being equal, starboard tack is then the favoured tack for progressing upwind in these gusty conditions (port tack in the Southern Hemisphere).

These stronger gusts, which we shall call 'air mass gusts', arrive from a near-windward direction. Some notice may be obtained from observing the behaviour of boats farther to windward or the more agitated water surface (catspaws). Since cruising yachts will be already reefed down to accommodate these gusts, no action is required other than to point up as the gust arrives if beating on starboard tack, and perhaps to go about before the gust arrives if beating on port tack (vice versa in the Southern Hemisphere). Similar gusts may be found in the vicinity of small or medium cumulus clouds (not producing showers). In fact, on otherwise windless days some wind will generally be found under scattered cumulus clouds.

Squalls
Quite a different and more dangerous type of gust occurs with heavy showers and thunderstorms associated with large cumulus and cumulonimbus clouds. These more vigorous and sometimes less predictable 'downdraft gusts' derive from the down rush of air accompanying heavy showers. If they last for more than one minute they are designated 'squalls'. The downdraft of air beats

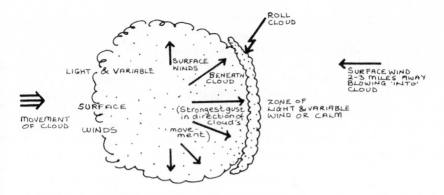

24a Storm cloud and surface winds, from above.

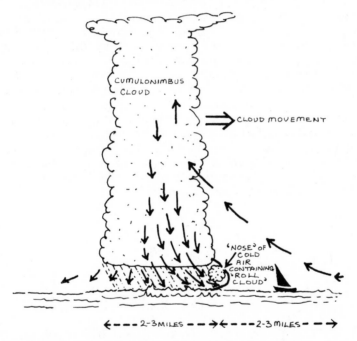

24b Downdraft and 'cold nose' in cumulonimbus storm cloud.

down on the surface and then fans out radially in the semicircle into which the rainstorm is moving: there is little downdraft effect to the rear of the storm (Diagram 24). The maximum force is directly ahead of the parent cloud.

Atmospheric pressure changes little with the approach of strong gusts and downdraft squalls, so the barometer will give no indication of their approach.

Avoiding such squalls requires deducing the track of the cumulonimbus cloud. It will be steered by the wind meaned over the whole depth of the cloud – at least several kilometres – which is frequently very different from the surface wind direction. To determine the track there is no substitute for taking frequent bearings of the middle of the shower, which will appear as a grey fuzziness beneath a dark cloud base against an otherwise fairly clear horizon. The surface wind itself is not a good indicator, as we shall soon see.

A well developed cumulonimbus cloud, capable of producing heavy showers or thunderstorms, affects the winds at surface level over a wide area in its vicinity, perhaps up to 5 miles in radius and sometimes more from the edge of the shower, which itself may be 5 to 10 miles across. Well ahead of the rainstorm, the surface wind blows gently towards it (Diagram 24). Within a mile or so of the edge of the storm this air rises away from the ground and eventually enters the storm cloud. There is then usually a zone of light and variable winds until the arrival of the storm cloud.

Meanwhile the downdraft from within the storm has formed a 'nose' of cold air just ahead of the storm edge, by friction at the ground surface (Diagram 25). The nose is an unstable condition since it contains cold (denser) air which is overlying less dense air and constantly seeks to descend to the surface. This occurs repeatedly, breaking down the nose only for it to be reformed by friction as the cold air continues to advance. The breakdown of the cold nose adds to the force of the squall.

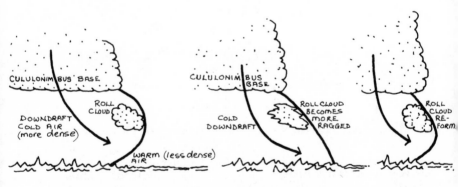

25 The downdraft 'cold nose' below cumulonimbus, which produces heavy gusts and squalls. It is constantly breaking down and re-forming (see text).

Roll cloud associated with an advancing squall at a distance of about a mile. The photograph shows the right-hand portion of the roll cloud only in order to highlight its characteristic bow shape. The turbulent 'ragged' appearance of the cloud's lower edge, estimated at 200 to 300 metres, is also typical. It is a clear indication of a strong, and often violent, sudden increase in wind speed within a few minutes. As this roll cloud arrived overhead the wind suddenly increased to 50 knots. (Photo courtesy R. J. Edwards)

A dark, arched roll of cloud, often visibly turbulent, develops within the nose of cold air and is often a very distinctive threatening feature which appears to race overhead on its final approach. Its arrival overhead coincides with the gust or squall: the wind may suddenly rise from near-calm to over 40 knots in a few seconds. Rain, often heavy, will follow almost immediately. The gust or squall soon drops to around half its original speed within a few minutes, and later as the rain eases the wind becomes quite light.

The first sign of the approach of such gusts is the roll-cloud. The second is the state of the sea underneath it and this is a good indication of the wind strength to come. However, the change in waves can normally only be seen when the storm is a mile away or closer. The speed of movement of the whole system is typically 25 knots (the range is probably from about 10 to perhaps 50 knots), so that at say half a mile there is normally a little over a minute before the squall hits, which may be just sufficient to reduce sail.

Though all roll-clouds when associated with heavy showers are clear harbingers of squalls, some roll-clouds which still look dark and threatening develop in front of clouds which are not producing (and never will produce) showers. As they arrive overhead there is little or no change in the already light wind. This non-starter is very difficult to pick out in advance, though the appearance of the sea underneath it will often give a clue: the only safe thing to do is to assume it will deliver a blow and at least reduce sail.

Similar squalls often occur at active cold fronts, but there the sudden increase of speed may well be accompanied by a veer (Northern Hemisphere) of about 90° in wind direction. Diagram 26 shows the position of the cold nose on the frontal boundary: its cycle of breakdown and redevelopment is similar to that in Diagram 25 and also strengthens the gusts as the front arrives. Incidentally, it is the leap-frogging effect of the repeated breakdown of the cold nose which chiefly accounts for a cold front

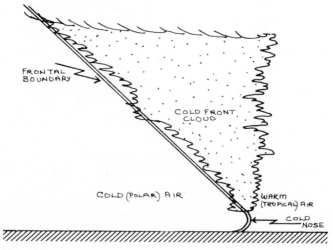

FRONTAL BOUNDARY

COLD FRONT CLOUD

COLD (POLAR) AIR

WARM (TROPICAL) AIR

COLD NOSE

26 The cold nose at a cold front boundary.

moving faster than the warm front ahead of it.

In some parts of the world cold fronts sweep across in advance of well known regional winds. For example the Norther of the Gulf of Mexico is the northerly behind a cold front; it usually occurs in winter. The Southerly Buster on the E coast of Australia is another post-cold front wind, as is the Pamperro off the E coast of South America which is perhaps the most notorious squall, sometimes exceeding 70 knots.

Cold front squalls take on the appearance of a line – that of the cold front. They are known as Line Squalls and the boundary is perpendicular to the direction of movement. Line squalls also occur independently of cold fronts. Though they may be found almost anywhere, they are more frequent in non-frontal troughs in temperate latitudes, and especially in the Doldrums. In fact, in the Doldrum zone most bad weather occurs as line squalls or in the Convergence Zones.

As a general guide it can perhaps be said that the faster the line squall is moving the stronger its winds will be, but this is not always the case. A 'weather eye constantly lifted' is all one can do in squally conditions and this means frequent all-round checks. At night, listen. Line squalls, as well as individual showers or thunderstorms, are clearly visible on properly adjusted 3 cm radar.

Local Wind Effects
Moving air takes the path of least resistance, tending to remain over the sea for as long as possible before it goes over the rougher land. As a result, wind blowing onshore at an angle will freshen near the coast, especially if it is formed by cliffs and particularly at a headland or cape, as these present a more effective barrier (Diagram 27a).

Air also tends to 'channel' along an estuary or any stretch of water between two land masses, for example on sea lochs or long lakes or the Solent. When the wind is already blowing along such a channel its speed over the water is higher than over the land on either side, due to 'funnelling'.

Some lakes and estuaries are so sheltered, especially in crosswinds, that only light winds are felt there even though a gale is blowing outside. Indeed, anchorages and harbours are usually chosen for their shelter from wind and waves, so learning to estimate the conditions 'outside' before leaving is very useful. This can be done from the speed of any low cloud which can be seen. By assuming that its movement represents the wind above the ground friction layer, a reasonable estimate of the surface wind can be made by backing the direction (anticlockwise) of movement about

$20°-30°$ and taking about 70% of the cloud speed. The skill can soon be acquired by practice: look at low-cloud movement from the land (particularly the coast) when strong winds are blowing, on as many different occasions as possible. This method is particularly successful if applied to the first traces to form of the cumulus caused by morning heating over the land.

Local Wave Effects
As waves reach shallow depths they can be seen to change their movement, so that the water moves more horizontally towards the shore as the wave approaches and back as it passes by. This can be verified by watching seaweed or flotsam in shallow water in fairly

27a Local wind effects found along sea coasts and the shores of rivers, lakes and estuaries.

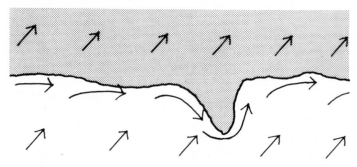

Deflection (bending) and freshening when wind blows obliquely onto the land.

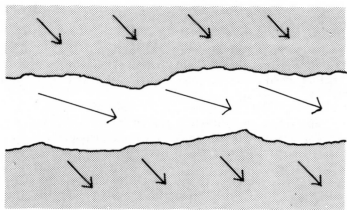

Shift of direction by channelling.

74

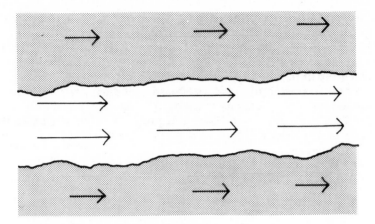

Funnelling increases the wind speed.

gentle conditions. The effect is also well known to swimmers, who suffer sometimes strong undertow as a breaker passes. Small boats landing or launching on the shore can be thrown back and pulled out with surprising force.

Due to bottom drag, waves slow down as they approach the shore, becoming shorter and steeper until they become unstable and break at the crests. The inshore ends of waves running obliquely towards the shore, or even perpendicular to it, are slowed more by friction on the bottom and thus are bent (refracted) so that they finally run almost parallel to a straight, gently shelving beach before they finally break (Diagram 27b). They are similarly bent round a headland to run into a bay which otherwise offers shelter from the wind.

Waves may also be refracted around islands to meet and produce chaotic and potentially dangerous wave patterns on the downwind side. A submerged bank (depth less than $\frac{1}{2}$ wavelength) also produces this effect and in rough seas will produce dangerous seas in its lee. The loss of at least one North Sea trawler has been attributed to this effect close to the Dogger Bank.

Sea and Land Breezes

Both sea and land breezes occur when there is already little wind over the area, which in turn is due to slack pressure gradients. Under clear skies the land warms up much more than the sea during the day and cools down much more at night. Strong surface heating during the day results in a pressure gradient perpendicular to the coast, with higher pressure over the sea and lower pressure over the land. A compensating onshore breeze (i.e. blowing from water to land) develops by late morning in temperate latitudes, say after 11 a.m. sun time (on some tropical coasts its arrival at a little after 10 a.m. can often be relied upon) and normally ceases around dusk when the initiating temperature contrast is destroyed. This is the sea breeze. It typically reaches Force 4 or 5 during the afternoon, though on some occasions when there is already a light offshore breeze it may only reach Force 3. It probably originates up to 10 miles or so offshore. The sea breeze is not confined to coasts; the

27b Wave refraction. The initial, offshore wave direction is shown by the arrow at the right.

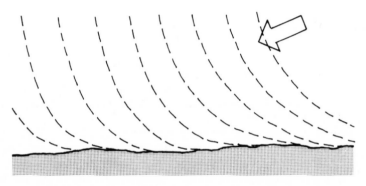

Onto a beach. The unrefracted waves might be a mile out.

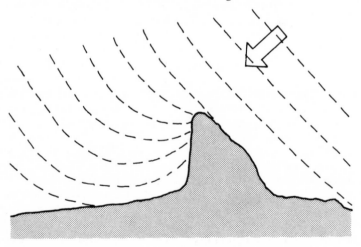

Around a headland.

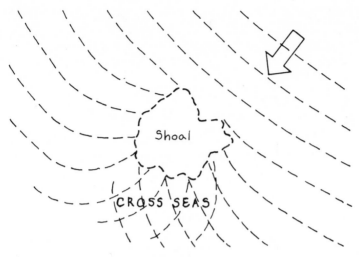

In the lee of an island or a shallow patch.

effect is also regularly observed on the shores of lakes that are at least a few miles across. The direction is normally perpendicular to the predominant coastal direction, though it tends to veer 20° to 30° (Northern Hemisphere) due to the deflection resulting from the earth's rotation. However, the sea breeze is sometimes very localized, especially in the initial stages. For example, the author has observed yachts off the Isle of Wight shore of the Solent sailing to an onto-the-Island sea breeze while simultaneously others on the mainland Hampshire side were sailing to an onshore breeze there on a pure sea breeze day. Later, the main N-going sea breeze from the S side of the Isle of Wight dominated over the whole area just as though the Solent had never existed as a sea breeze producing area.

The land breeze, also occurring under clear sky and light wind conditions, usually sets in during the late evening and dies away at sunrise. It results from higher pressure over the land and lower pressure over the sea at night and blows off the land. It is usually much more gentle than the sea breeze, averaging around Force 3, and extends several miles offshore.

The land sea breeze regime is so regular in some parts of the tropics that fishermen in small outrigger canoes sail out a few miles before daybreak with the last of the land breeze and then, after fishing for a few hours, sail home on the sea breeze during the afternoon.

Sea and land breezes make sailing along coasts a possibility when farther offshore calms may persist for days. This is particularly so in parts of the Mediterranean in summer.

BEAUFORT WIND SCALE AND ASSOCIATED WAVE HEIGHTS

Scale no.	General Description	Appearance of the Sea
0	Calm	Sea like a mirror.
1	Light Air	Ripples with the appearance of scales are formed without foam crests.
	Light Breeze	Small wavelets, still short but more pronounced. Crests have a glassy appearance and do not break.
3	Gentle Breeze	Large wavelets. Crests begin to break. Foam of glassy appearance. Perhaps scattered white horses.
4	Moderate Breeze	Small waves, becoming longer; fairly frequent white horses.
5	Fresh Breeze	Moderate waves, taking a more pronounced long form; many white horses are formed. Chance of some spray.
6	Strong Breeze	Large waves begin to form; the white foam crests are more extensive everywhere. Probably some spray.
7	Near Gale	Sea heaps up and white foam from breaking waves begins to be blown in streaks along the direction of the wind.
8	Gale	Moderately high waves of greater length; edges of crests begin to break into the spin-drift. The foam is blown in well-marked streaks along the direction of the wind.
9	Strong Gale	High waves. Dense streaks of foam along the direction of the wind. Crests of waves begin to topple, tumble and roll over. Spray may affect visibility.
10	Storm	Very high waves with long overhanging crests. The resulting form in great patches is blown in dense white streaks along the direction of the wind. On the whole the surface takes on a white appearance. The tumbling of the sea becomes heavy and shock-like. Visibility affected.
11	Violent Storm	Exceptionally high waves (small and medium sized ships might be for a time lost to view behind waves). The sea is completely covered with long white patches of foam lying along the direction of the wind. Everywhere the edges of the wave crests are blown into froth. Visibility affected.
12	Hurricane	The air is filled with foam and spray. Sea completely white with driving spray; visibility very seriously affected.

TABLE 4 Wave heights are based on wave recorder statistics. Since maximum wave height depends on wind duration as well as speed, maximums for various durations are given. Should a depression move at the same speed as the waves, then the 'duration' is considerable; in

Wind Speed*		Wave Heights (metres)				
Range (knots)	Mean (knots)	Average height	Max. 10 min. period	Max. any 6 hr period	Max. any 48 hr period	Scale no.
1	0	—	—	—	—	0
1-3	2	—	—	—	—	1
4-6	5	—	—	—	—	2
7–10	9	0.5	0.8	—	—	3
11-16	13	1.1	1.8	2.4	2.7	4
17-21	19	2.0	3.2	4.4	5.0	5
22-27	24	3.1	5.0	6.8	7.5	6
28-33	30	4.5	7.2	9.9	10.9	7
34-40	37	6.7	10.7	14.7	16.3	8
41-47	44	9.3	14.9	20.4	22.6	9
48-55	52	12.3	19.7	27.0	29.9	10
56-63	60	15.5	24.8	34.0	37.7	11
64 and over	?	?	?	?	?	12

these circumstances very large waves will arrive *simultaneously* with a very strong wind.

*To convert m/sec into knots, multiply by 2.

Katabatic Wind

Like a land breeze this is a night-time effect due to cooling of the land surface. It is a hill and valley wind caused by the air in contact with the cooling slopes itself being cooled and, on becoming more dense, sinking to the floor of the valley. If the valley floor itself slopes to the shore then the cold air flows down the slope and eventually out to sea. Katabatic winds are stronger in mountainous areas and their effect off the coast will be more noticeable where the mountains or hills are close to the shore. Under these conditions a katabatic wind may reach Force 5 to 6 close to the coast, gradually decreasing as it fans out to dissipate its momentum by about 5 miles out to sea. It also occurs on a smaller scale on lakes with hilly shores.

Beaufort Scale

Originally devised by Admiral Beaufort early in the 19th century as a means of estimating the strength of wind at sea, this related a scale of numbers from 0 to 12 to the maximum amount of sail that a ship of the line of that time could carry, and to the appearance of the sea. It was later defined in terms of wind speed in knots (Table 4). (Speeds in metres per second m/sec can be converted into knots by multiplying by 2.) The average and maximum wave heights are different from the values given before 1982 (and still found in some books). The revised heights are based on wave recorder data and are more representative of actual sea conditions.

ELEVEN
Weather Forecasts and Maps

Forecasts appearing in the press and broadcast on television and radio originate from the national meteorological centre whose responsibility it is to provide weather information for the country. Since national practices vary to some extent, those used in the United Kingdom will be explained, though they may be taken as fairly representative.

A vast amount of weather information is received from numerous land stations and ships around the globe, some producing balloon-borne soundings of the atmosphere, from aircraft on international routes and from earth-orbiting satellites. This information is analysed at Bracknell, the British national centre, by a very powerful computer which produces forecast data covering the greater part of the globe for several days ahead. These numerical predictions form the basis of the forecast charts which are then produced several times each day.

Forecasts appearing in newspapers are short verbal accounts compiled for land-based activities and may be of limited use for marine pursuits, but some also print actual and forecast weather charts. Due to newspaper printing and distribution constraints, however, these charts have originated from Bracknell during the previous afternoon: nevertheless they are useful in indicating the presence and movements of depressions, anticyclones and fronts.

The presentations given on television vary, but most will display a chart and describe the development and movements of weather features. These forecasts, though much more up to date than newspaper forecasts, are also primarily meant for land-based pursuits though some regions give information on expected winds on nearby coasts.

Most radio forecasts are also aimed at a shore-based audience, but a special Shipping Forecast for vessels at sea in a fairly wide area centred on the British isles and reaching NW Europe (Diagram 28) is broadcast on BBC Radio 4 (200 kHz/1500 m) at 0033, 0555, 1355 and 1750 each day. Parts of these forecasts are also transmitted by the Coast Radio Stations operated by BT, and by some local radio stations at other times (listed in nautical almanacs and the Admiralty List of Radio Signals ALRS Vol. 3).

The boundaries and names of forecast areas used by other national maritime meteorological services are given in *Meteorology at Sea* (pub. Stanford Maritime).

The Bracknell shipping forecaster's 'horizon' lies thousands of miles away since he is able to study the weather developments over a vast section of the Northern Hemisphere and to predict dramatic and often dangerous deteriorations in the weather long before there is any sign of such a change in the sky, the wind or the barometer to those at sea. There is no substitute to listening to each shipping forecast and, in a rapidly developing situation, to monitoring the gale warnings (see below). To ignore shipping forecasts continually will eventually put the craft and her crew at unjustifiably high risk. Each severe storm produces a list of casualties among yachts and other vessels; in nearly all these cases the storm was adequately forecast by the Meteorological Office at Bracknell, sometimes days ahead. In more than a few, attention to these forecasts would have avoided disaster.

Due to the limited broadcast time available, the shipping forecast is prepared in a condensed 'telegraphic' style and the content is always presented in the same order. First comes a listing of all the sea areas in which **gale warnings** are in operation. This is followed by the **general synopsis** which is an account of the development and movement of depressions and anticyclones and, when time permits, of fronts, affecting the sea areas around the British Isles and NW Europe. **Forecasts by sea areas** are given next, some grouped together but always following the same order which is roughly clockwise around the British Isles beginning with Viking to the NE and finishing with SE Iceland. The forecast by areas gives the expected wind directions and Beaufort forces and changes; then the weather (fair, rain, snow, etc); and lastly the visibility for the 24-hour period following the time of broadcast. Then comes a list of **actual weather observations** for a number of 'coastal' locations around Britain. The coast stations which are used change from time to time, so they are all shown in Diagram 28.

The speed of movement of the lows and highs is given in the general synopsis either by 'from' and 'to' positions or by the use of certain descriptive terms which, in this context, have much more

28 UK Shipping Forecast areas and coastal stations. Not all the stations report at any one time, so a full list is given here for reference.

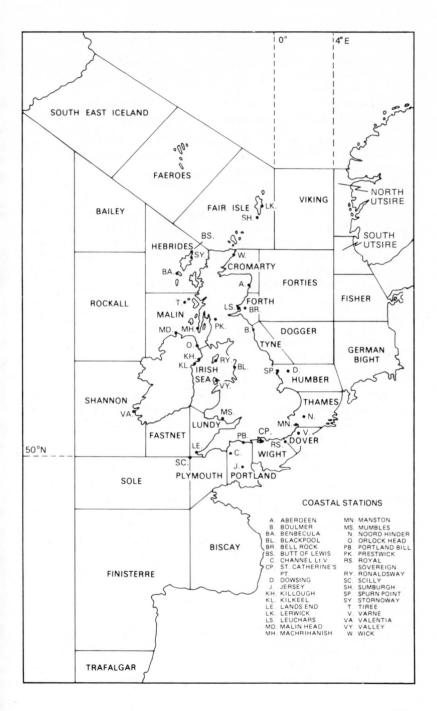

COASTAL STATIONS

A.	ABERDEEN	MN.	MANSTON
B.	BOULMER	MS.	MUMBLES
BA.	BENBECULA	N.	NOORD HINDER
BL.	BLACKPOOL	O.	ORLOCK HEAD
BR.	BELL ROCK	PB.	PORTLAND BILL
BS.	BUTT OF LEWIS	PK.	PRESTWICK
C.	CHANNEL Lt.V.	RS.	ROYAL
CP.	ST. CATHERINE'S		SOVEREIGN
	PT.	RY.	RONALDSWAY
D.	DOWSING	SC.	SCILLY
J.	JERSEY	SH.	SUMBURGH
KH.	KILLOUGH	SP.	SPURN POINT
KL.	KILKEEL	SY.	STORNOWAY
LE.	LANDS END	T.	TIREE
LK.	LERWICK	V.	VARNE
LS.	LEUCHARS	VA.	VALENTIA
MD.	MALIN HEAD	VY.	VALLEY
MH.	MACHRIHANISH	W.	WICK

precise definitions than in common usage. These terms are:

Slowly	moving at less than 15 knots
Steadily	moving at 15 to 25 knots
Rather Quickly	moving at 25 to 35 knots
Rapidly	moving at 35 to 45 knots
Very Rapidly	moving at over 45 knots.

The forecast positions of depressions, though generally very accurate, should not be interpreted too precisely. After all, in the case of a low moving at 30 knots, an error of only 5° in predicting its expected track and 5 knots in its speed will mean that, after 24 hours, the low will be anywhere within 100 miles of its forecast position; e.g. if forecast to be in Dogger the low may finish up in any of the adjacent areas. This possibility should always be considered when a low is expected to move into a sea area within a few hundred miles of you, depending on its speed of travel, for the winds may turn out to be much stronger than forecast. As a general rule, only those features which are expected to influence the winds over the normal sea areas will be given in the general synopsis. However, if broadcast time permits, a depression which is expected to bring gales into several sea areas during the next 24 to 48 hour period may be included by way of early warning, even though it will be too far away to affect the winds in any area during the first 24 hours.

Winds given by areas in the main body of the shipping forecast will usually be stated in two parts, which may be interpreted as 'at first' and 'later', though sometimes more than one substantial wind change may be expected and the description will then be more complicated. If a low is expected to cross a given sea area the wind direction will be given as: 'cyclonic' (perhaps '6 to gale 8'). This means that the wind changes will be consistent with the counter-clockwise rotation around a depression. The light winds in anticyclones and ridges of high pressure and in other areas of slack pressure gradients such as cols will be described as 'variable 3 or less'. In describing wind speed, using the Beaufort Scale, the word 'Force' is omitted except in the case of 'hurricane Force 12' when it is included, by international agreement, to distinguish this from a tropical 'hurricane' (Chapter 13). However, by listening to earlier forecasts most sane people will be safely in harbour before such winds are predicted.

Weather is described very briefly as fair, rain, snow, drizzle, showers, or extensive fog as appropriate. 'Showers', which covers the whole range from light showers to thunderstorms, are localized and typically last for half an hour or so, whereas 'rain' means widespread and continuous precipitation associated with fronts and depressions. When strong winds are otherwise not forecast, 'squally showers' may be used. This should be understood to mean that gusts or squalls associated with the showers will far exceed the forecast wind speed, and will typically reach 30 knots and sometimes much more (see Chapter 10).

Visibility is always given last in the forecast by areas. The descriptive terms used have precise definitions:

Good	means more than 5 nautical miles
Moderate	means 2 to 5 n. miles
Poor	means 1,000 m to 2 n. miles
Fog	means less than 1,000 metres.

Variations in visibility commonly occur at sea even over the small sea areas such as Dover. Consequently the forecast visibility is often given as a range, e.g. 'moderate or good' or perhaps 'moderate or poor'. Since sea fog is often very patchy in nature, the visibility may be described as 'moderate with fog patches' which implies that about 20% of the area may be fog-covered. 'Poor with fog banks' may be used with fog covering about 20 to 40% of the surface, and 'extensive fog' with more than 40% of the surface expected to be fog-covered. In the absence of rain, etc the weather will be described as 'fair' even when the visibility includes fog patches or banks, but weather and visibility are combined when 'extensive fog' is forecast. 'Showers. Good.' implies that the visibility will be good except for local deteriorations in the showers.

Coastal station reports are presented in a slightly diffferent form. They give, in order: wind direction (32-point compass e.g. North by East), wind speed (Beaufort Force), weather if significant (rain, showers, etc), visibility in miles down to 1 nautical mile then in metres, barometric pressure in whole millibars, and lastly the 'pressure tendency' which is the pressure change during the 3-hour period immediately before the time of the observation. The terms used to describe the pressure tendency also have precise meanings:

Falling (or Rising) Slowly	means 0.1 to 1.5 mb change
Falling (Rising)	means 1.6 to 3.5 mb change
Falling (Rising) Quickly	means 3.6 to 6.0 mb change
Falling (Rising) Very Rapidly	means more than 6 mb change

Clearly the last two are significant, particularly with falling pressure, for they probably indicate that strong winds or gales will follow (Chapter 8).

Another service for vessels at sea is the Forecast for Inshore Waters (up to 12 miles offshore from coasts and islands), broadcast on Radio 4 (200 kHz) at 0038 immediately following the Shipping Forecast, and on Radio 3 (1215 kHz) at 0655. It is presented in a similar style to the shipping forecast and has its own list of coastal station reports.

Several local radio stations broadcast special forecasts for their coastal regions, particularly in the sailing season (see almanacs and local papers). Also, British Telecom currently provides an automatic telephone service 'Marineline' which gives forecasts, updated several times each day, for coastal waters around the UK. The service for much of the Channel coast will cover waters across to the French coast over an area which closely approximates to sea areas Dover, Wight and Portland. In the absence of this service a forecast may be obtained by telephone from your local Weather Centre, if necessary by radio link through the nearest Coast Radio Station.

Gale warnings, also originated by the shipping forecaster at Bracknell, are broadcast on Radio 4 at the first programme break following their receipt and also at the end of the next hourly news bulletin. It is well worth listening to Radio 4 'on the hour' for new gale warnings that may be issued between shipping forecasts as they may give hours more time to alter plans, as well as providing insurance against accidentally missing the next forecast. Coast Radio Stations also broadcast gale warnings for adjacent sea areas soon after receiving them.

Gale warnings are issued from Bracknell whenever the wind speed is expected to exceed 33 knots. That is the *mean* wind speed averaged over several minutes not the gusts, which commonly exceed the mean speed by 25 to 50% and sometimes by more than 100%. Definitions used and their limits are:

Gale Force 8	34 to 40 knots
Severe Gale Force 9	41 to 47 knots
Storm Force 10	48 to 55 knots
Violent Storm Force 11	56 to 63 knots
Hurricane Force 12	64 knots or over.

The time of issue from Bracknell and an indication of the time of onset of the gales, based on this time of issue, is also included using the following terms:

Imminent	within 6 hours of the time of issue
Soon	6 to 12 hours from the time of issue
Later	more than 12 hours from the time of issue.

When there is a small possibility of a gale towards the end of the shipping forecast period, though the confidence of its occurring is too low to justify the issue of a 'later' warning, the possibility is indicated by 'perhaps gale 8 later'.

Every effort is made to give as much warning as possible. Warnings are also issued for changes of wind direction of more than 45° and for reductions below Force 9 or above. No warning is given of decreases below Force 8 other than the text of the area forecasts. Instead, a statement is made when the gale has ceased, e.g. 'Hebrides. Gales now ceased.' Though these cancellations are transmitted by the Coast Radio Stations, surprisingly they are not broadcast by the BBC. If a new gale is expected to arrive 6 to 12 hours after the old gale has ceased, the relevant warning takes the form 'Plymouth, Biscay. Gales now ceased. Southerly gales Force 8 expected soon.' These new warnings are issued by the BBC and Coast Radio Stations. When the duration of the expected reduction below gale strength between old and new gales is less than 6 hours, no cancellation is given but a warning for the new gale direction will be given if appropriate. On any occasion when a gale warning does not seem consistent with an earlier one, consider that the later issue updates the earlier.

Warnings of **strong winds reaching Force 6** (22 knots) are issued for the areas up to 5 miles offshore by local radio stations, collectively covering the UK coastline, for the season Good Friday to 31 October. The warning, including its time of issue from the local Weather Centre, is broadcast at the first programme break and also after the next hourly news bulletin.

TWELVE
Drawing Met Maps

It is often the case at sea that some operation, whether sail-changing or trimming or collision avoidance, occurs at shipping forecast time and the forecast is missed. To avoid this, it is a good idea to carry a radio with tape recorder which can be set up in good time, perhaps initiated by an alarm. The forecast may then be listened to when the excitement is over. A cassette recorder is also useful for constructing your own met-map. It is extremely valuable to have an up-to-date picture of the 'general synopsis', and the ability to do this is a requirement of the RYA examinations.

In most cases shipping forecasts will be substantially correct, but due to the complex problems associated with predicting the behaviour of the atmosphere, in particular the development and movement of its transient eddies (depressions), some forecasts will be incorrect. Normally the inaccuracies will have been detected by the time the next forecast is issued about 6 hour later. The prudent course, especially for small, slower craft, is to take down each shipping forecast and also to monitor the weather signs and changes in the interval before the next forecast by 'lifting a weather eye' (see Chapters 5 and 8).

This observation, of course, reveals changes in one's immediate vicinity. A more general check on the forecast may be made by plotting a weather chart using later information than that on which the shipping forecast is based, by working from the coastal station reports which are normally made 4 to 6 hours later than the time of the general synopsis in winter and 3 to 5 hours during BST, depending on the time of the broadcast. Though the general synopsis is based on a chart for some 6 to 8 hours earlier than the radio broadcast time, in constructing the shipping forecast by areas the Met Office forecaster will have taken account of more recent observations of actual conditions. Nevertheless, the broadcast coastal station reports are not normally to hand, due to transmission delays, by the time compilation of the shipping forecast has been completed. A new chart produced on board, for the time of the coastal station reports of actual conditions, therefore provides an invaluable check on the expected developments detailed in the general synopsis.

Writing down shipping forecasts will be made much easier if specially prepared forms are used. A number now available, published by the Meteorological Office, the Royal Meteorological Society and the RYA (among others), display the forecast areas and coastal stations in map and tabulated form which makes for rapid entry of the data. Whether you use prepared forms, a notebook or anything else, it *is* important to *write it down*. It is surprising how a group of people all eagerly listening can disagree afterwards about exactly what was said; and also how easy it is to fall behind the broadcaster without practice. Get your crew to write it down too, for practice. However, the brain plays tricks and only a tape recording will resolve different versions.

Since the forecast is read out at normal speed and not dictation speed, some form of shorthand will have to be used. Wind direction, weather and visibility can be reduced to initials, e.g. W or W'ly for west or westerly, R for rain, M for moderate visibility; as these elements are always broadcast in a set order there should be no ambiguity. The passage of time may be indicated by an arrow, and wind direction changes by a counterclockwise or clockwise arrow. For example, 'Irish Sea. South 6 to gale 8 veering west 5. Rain then showers. Moderate or poor becoming good' may be reduced to:

$$\text{S } 6\text{-}8 \; \curvearrowright\!\text{W5} \cdot\!\rightarrow \dot{\diamond} \; \text{MP} \rightarrow \text{G}$$

When a depression is expected to pass over a given area the forecast wind direction will be given as 'cyclonic'. This, and the associated wind force, say 'Cyclonic 6–8', may be entered as

$$\widehat{6\text{-}8}$$

Similar abbreviations to those in the shipping forecast may be used for the coastal station reports, but some additional ones will have to be included particularly for 'pressure tendency'. This is perhaps most easily recorded as a symbol representing the slope of a graph of pressure against time, as shown in Table 6 and the following examples:

'Dowsing. South 2. Fog. 300 metres, 1016. Steady.' may be shortened to:

$$\text{S2 } \text{F } 300 \; 1016 -$$

'Tiree. Southeast 8. Continuous heavy rain. 2 miles. 993. Falling very rapidly' to:

$$\text{SE8 } \text{HR } 2 \; 993 \; \backslash$$

Timing

Having taken down the complete shipping forecast, it is important to understand the four time references that have been used. Firstly, the forecast is for the 24-hour period from the initial Radio 4 broadcast time (the coast radio stations and some local radio stations repeat parts of this forecast 2 or 3 hours later). Secondly, it will have been issued by the shipping forecaster at Bracknell about an hour earlier. The general synopsis will have been based on the last available analysed chart for the whole Atlantic and European areas, drawn every 6 hours, usually 6 to 8 hours before broadcast time. Lastly, the coastal station reports will have been made 4 to 6 hours *later* than the time of the analysed chart.

For example, a typical forecast broadcast on Radio 4 at *1355* would be read like this.

'Here is the shipping forecast issued by the Meteorological Office at *1305* on Wednesday 5th February . . . There are warnings of gales in Viking . . . The general synopsis at *0600*. Low Fair Isle . . . The area forecasts for the next 24 hours . . . And now the coastal station reports for *1200*. Tiree . . .'

Local clock time is always used in the shipping forecast. Since most of these time references are already local clock times, they remain unchanged in summer time. However, analysed chart times at Bracknell are always GMT, so if our example had been dated July, it would have read 'The general synopsis at 0700. Low . . .'.

Constructing a Met-map

After writing down the forecast, the next step in the production of your own met-map is to plot the *coastal station reports* (not to be confused with sea area forecasts). Remember that the time of this chart will be that of the coastal station reports. The following system is a simplified variation of that used in professional meteorological practice.

Wind direction, which is that from which the wind is blowing, should be plotted as an arrow pointing towards the reporting station; each Beaufort Force is plotted as half a feather on the 'clockwise' end of the shaft, e.g.

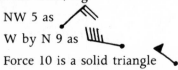

NW 5 as

W by N 9 as

Force 10 is a solid triangle

Weather should be plotted on the left-hand side of the reporting station (or as near as the wind plot will allow) using the shorthand symbols shown in Table 5. A distinction between 'intermittent' (began less than 1 hour ago) and 'continuous' precipitation is made in meteorological practice, but for the purposes of this discussion there is little benefit from adopting it here. Note that intermittent precipitation differs from showers in that the former falls from layer cloud (nimbostratus) while the latter falls from convective cloud (cumulonimbus), though their durations may be similar.

	Slight	Moderate	Heavy	Showers
Rain	•	• •	• • •	• ▽
Drizzle	،	، ،	، ، ،	
Snow	✳	✳ ✳	✳ ✳ ✳	✳ ▽

Hail	Thunderstorm	Fog	Distant Fog	Mist	Haze
△̱ ▽	℞	≡	(≡)	＝	∞

TABLE 5   Symbols for plotting precipitation.

FALLING			RISING	
Description	Symbol	Change in last 3 hours	Description	Symbol
Steady	―			
Now falling	⌃		Now rising	⌄
Falling more slowly	⌐		Rising more slowly	⌐
Falling slowly	⁀	0.1 to 0.5 mb	Rising slowly	⁀
Falling	⟍	1.6 to 3.5 mb	Rising	⟋
Falling quickly	⟍	3.6 to 6.0 mb	Rising quickly	⟋
Falling very rapidly	＼	6.1 mb	Rising very rapidly	／

TABLE 6   Plotting symbols for barometric tendency.

Visibility should be plotted on the left-hand side of the station outside the weather symbol. If necessary add **m** for metres and **NM** or **M** for nautical miles, though there should be no ambiguity since short distances in metres will be accompanied by a fog symbol (see examples below).

Pressure is plotted top right and pressure **tendency** on the right-hand side of the station, using the symbols shown in Table 6.

The following examples of typical reports show their notation and plotting symbols. They are shown first as they would be broadcast, then as written down by a listener, and finally as plotted on a map. After a little practice the second stage may be eliminated and the coastal stations plotted directly from the radio or cassette. Your own weather observations for the same time should also be plotted.

Butt of Lewis. North 4. 15 miles. Showers. 1007. Now rising.

$$\text{N4 15 R Sh 1007} \quad \backslash\!/ \qquad 15\,\dot{\triangledown}\;\ulcorner^{1007}_{\ \ \backslash\!/}$$

Bell Rock. South 5. 3 miles. Continuous slight rain. 999. Falling more quickly.

$$\text{S5 3 SR 999} \quad \backslash \qquad 3\,\overset{\bullet\;\bullet}{\underset{\equiv}{\bullet}}\,^{999}\,\backslash$$

Scillies. Southwest by west 2. 100 metres. Fog. 1016. Falling slowly.

$$\text{SW'W 2 100 F 1016} \quad \backslash \qquad 100\,\equiv_{\bullet}\!\overset{1016}{\underset{\smile}{\backslash}}$$

To make the plot more complete, the 'at first' forecast winds should be plotted in their appropriate sea areas as representative of the winds over the open sea at the time of the coastal reports. Now plot any information from the general synopsis such as the positions of highs, lows, etc after allowing for the time interval between the time of the general synopsis and that of the coastal station reports, as follows. (This information should be entered lightly in pencil since it may be adjusted later.)

The general synopsis will give the position of a high or low at a stated initial time and again at the final time some 24 hours later. In constructing our met-map for the time of the coastal station reports, some 4–6 hours later than the initial time, we shall have to interpolate its position and central pressure. For example, 'At 1200, low Sole 973 expected Dogger 990 by 1200 tomorrow' indicates, after plotting the first position in the middle of Sole and the last position in the middle of Dogger, that the low is moving NE at about 25 knots. We require its position at 1600 (the time of the coastal station reports), i.e. some 4 hours after the first position. We are given the movement over 24 hours, so we may derive the 1600 position by moving NE from the initial position in Sole some 100 miles (4 × 25); or we may interpolate this position by applying 4/24ths of the given total movement in 24 hours from the initial position.

The central pressure of the low is expected to rise from 973 to 990 mb in the 24 hours, i.e. by 17 mb. Assume a constant rate of filling and take 4/24ths of the rise and add this to the initial pressure: thus 4/24 × 17 = 3, therefore the central pressure at 1600 is 976 mb.

Again, the general synopsis may state 'Atlantic low moving steadily northeast expected Hebrides 987 by 1800 tomorrow.' If we were to produce a met-map for 2300 hours (the time of the coastal station reports given with the 0033 shipping forecast) we can deduce a position for the low at 2300 as follows. We are given the final position of the low and an indication of its speed ('steadily' means 15 to 25 knots – see previous Chapter). Using 20 knots as its speed for 19 hours (the difference between the time of our met-map and of the final position of the low), we can derive an approximate position at 2300 hours some 380 miles or so SW of the centre of sea area Hebrides. Since we are not told whether the low is deepening or filling, assume it is in a 'steady state'. If it was said to be deepening then an adjustment would have to be made. We can only guess at an 'average' rate of deepening, say 15 mb in 24 hours (though it may be considerably more). This gives about 10 mb in 19 hours, so the central pressure at 2300 hours would be approximately 997 mb.

Next sketch in the isobars (lines joining places of equal pressure), remembering that the winds at sea are very roughly parallel to the isobars such that in the Northern Hemisphere the low pressure is on the left hand when running with the wind (on the right in the Southern Hemisphere). (Sometimes the wind at the coastal stations may be almost perpendicular to the isobars, however, due to land topography, land and see breezes.) When sketching the first isobar, select a value which is common to at least two coastal stations and then sketch in the remainder at 2 mb (even) intervals according to the pressures and winds at the remaining coastal stations and winds over the sea areas.

The R.Met.Soc/RYA form includes a scale for estimating Beaufort wind force from isobar spacing. This may be used in reverse to determine the isobar spacing over the sea from the 'at first' forecast winds. Place one point of the dividers on the extreme left hand of the scale marked Beaufort force and the other on the forecast Beaufort number. Once set, the dividers are than transferred to the appropriate sea area to give the isobar spacing. The positions of fronts may be deduced by using Table 1, on weather changes associated with fronts (pages 49–50). Adjust the light sketching of the position of isobars and fronts until they comply with all the information given in the forecast and with that in Table 1. Then draw them in more boldly.

Drawing Your Own Maps
The following examples of met-maps produced from shipping forecasts will amplify the description just given. It is well worth working these through, using the diagrams afterwards to check your notation and plotting and your final map. *Note*: the three Examples are not related to each other.

Example 1
Shipping Forecast issued by the Meteorological Office at 0505 on Saturday, 2nd November.

There are warnings of gales in Viking, North Utsire, South Utsire, Forties, Cromarty, Forth, Tyne, Dogger, Fisher, German Bight, Humber, Thames, Finisterre, Irish Sea, Malin, Hebrides, Fair Isle, Faeroes and SE Iceland.

The general synopsis at midnight.
Low 300 miles N of Viking 974 slow moving, filling 978 by midnight tonight. New low moving steadily SE expected 200 miles S of Iceland 994 by same time. Low near Finisterre 1002 moving slowly NE with little change.

The area forecasts for the next 24 hours.
Viking, North Utsire, South Utsire. NW 7 to severe gale 9 occasionally storm 10 in Viking at first. Squally wintry showers. Moderate or good.
Forties, Cromarty. NW backing W 7 to severe gale 9, decreasing 6. Squally wintry showers. Moderate or good.
Forth, Tyne. NW 6 to gale 8 backing W 5. Wintry showers. Good.
Dogger, Fisher, German Bight. NW 6 to gale 8, occasionally severe gale 9 in Fisher and perhaps later in Dogger and German Bight. Squally wintry showers. Moderate or good.

29 First plotting stage (see Example 1 in text). The form shown is the Royal Meteorological Society/RYA Metmap, which on the back is designed for taking down broadcast forecasts and station reports.

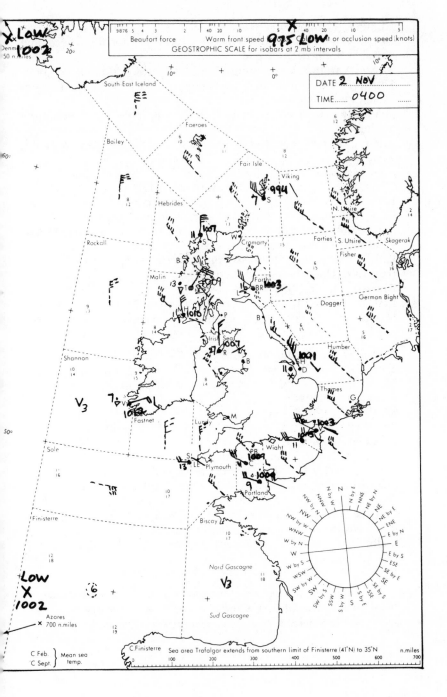

Humber, Thames. NW 6 occasionally gale 8. Showers. Good.
Dover, Wight, Portland, Plymouth. NW 5 occasionally 6 becoming variable 3. Showers. Good.
Biscay. Variable 3 becoming SE 5. Rain later. Moderate or good.
Finisterre. Cyclonic 6 occasionally gale 8. Occasional rain. Moderate.
Sole. E'ly 5 or 6 occasionally 7 in S. Rain later. Good becoming moderate.
Lundy, Fastnet. N'ly 4 or 5 becoming variable 3. Showers. Good.
Irish Sea. NW 6 occasionally gale 8 at first in N, decreasing 3. Showers. Good.
Shannon. Variable 3 or 4. Showers. Moderate or good.
Rockall. N'ly backing SW'ly 4 or 5, occasionally 6 at first and again later. Showers then rain. Good becoming moderate.
Malin, Hebrides. NW 6 occasionally gale 8 at first, backing SW 4 or 5. Wintry showers at first. Good.
Bailey. N 6 backing SE 4 increasing 6, perhaps gale 8 later. Showers then rain. Good becoming moderate.
Fair Isle, Faeroes. NW'ly 7 to severe gale 9 occasionally storm 10 at first, decreasing 6. Squally wintry showers. Moderate or good.
SE Iceland. N 6 occasionally gale 8 at first, becoming variable 3 then E 6 or 7. Wintry showers at first. Good. Light icing in N.

And now the coastal station reports for 0400 GMT.
Tiree. NNE 6. Showers. 13 miles. 1009. Now rising.
Butt of Lewis. N by E 7. Recent rain and snow. 11 miles. 1007. Falling more slowly.
Sumburgh. NW 8. Recent hail. 7 miles. 994. Falling quickly.
Bell Rock. NW by W 6. 16 miles. 1003. Rising slowly.
Dowsing. NNW 8. Slight rain and snow. 11 miles. 1001. Now rising.
Varne. WNW 6. 11 miles. 1003. Falling slowly.
Royal Sovereign. W 6. 11 miles. 1005. Falling more slowly.
Channel Light Vessel. WNW 6. 11 miles. 1009. Falling more slowly.
Scilly. 0300 GMT. W 4. 13 miles. 1011. Falling slowly.
Valentia. ENE 4. Showers. 7 miles. 1012. Falling more slowly.
Ronaldsway. N 3. 27 miles. 1007. Rising slowly.
Malin Head. N by W 6. Recent showers. 16 miles. 1010. Falling slowly.
Jersey. W by N. 9 miles. 1009. Falling slowly.

The coastal station reports for 0400 on 2 November are shown in Diagram 29a. The 'at first' winds (meaned if necessary) for each sea area and information from the general synopsis have also been

29b Drawing in the first isobars.

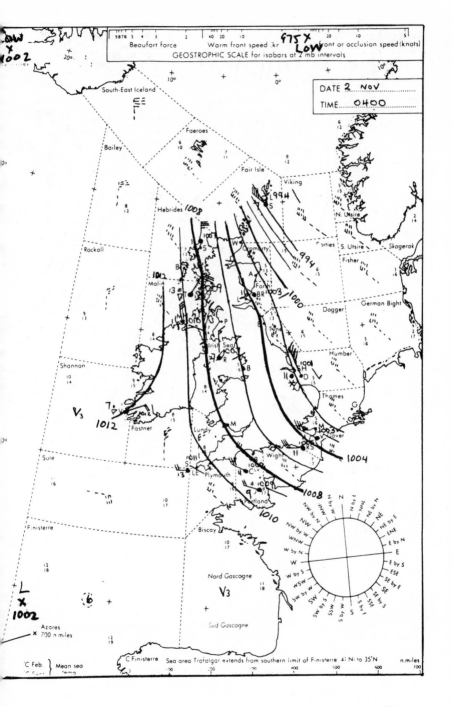

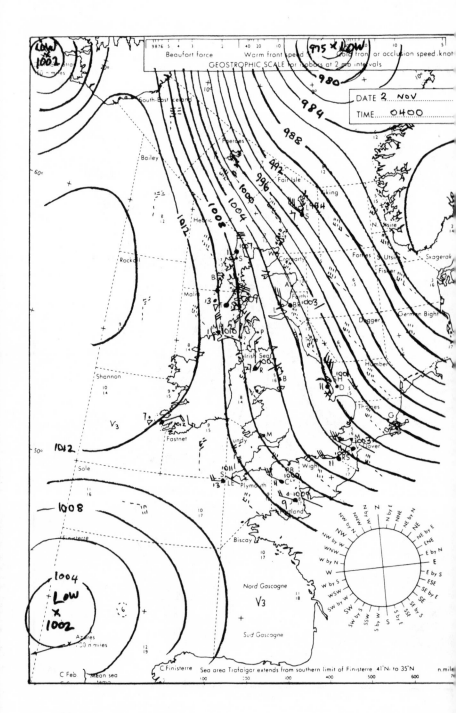

plotted. We need to know the positions of the lows at 0400 (the time of the met-map). Since the low N of Viking is slow-moving, it will require no adjustment for position but its central pressure will change to 975 mb (1/6 of the total change). The Iceland low is moving steadily, at say 20 knots, SE. If we backtrack NW for 20 hours from the forecast position, the low will be located in the Denmark Straits at 0400 with pressure of, say, 1002 mb (though it may not have formed by this time). In the SW, the low on the W side of Finisterre is moving slowly NE into this sea area. It is enough here to move it just inside the W boundary of Finisterre. Since none of these estimated positions for the lows lie near the reporting coastal stations, we can make no further adjustments to them.

Isobars are drawn at 2 mb intervals, e.g. 998, 1000, 1002 etc. Remembering that winds blow roughly parallel to the isobars and give an anti-clockwise circulation around a low, examining the winds and plotted pressures will reveal that the isobars will run from the NW to the SE across most of the map. So start in the NW of Britain and look for pressure values which are nearly equal (isobars join places of equal pressure) as the eye scans SE across the country. The observations from the Butt of Lewis, Tiree, Malin Head, Ronaldsway, Channel Light Vessel and Jersey are all within 1 mb of 1008. The first isobar to be drawn in then should be the 1008 mb isobar. This should be followed by the 1004 isobar using Bell Rock, Varne and Royal Sovereign. Both isobars are shown more boldly on Diagram 29b.

Complete the drawing of isobars over the British Isles from the remainder of the coastal station reports: note that the ENE wind at Valentia will require the 1012 isobar over W Ireland to run away SW over Shannon. The isobars may now be drawn over the sea areas with the help of dividers and the Beaufort scale at the top of the chart, which will give an approximation to the isobar spacing for the forecast winds (Diagram 29c).

Example 2
The Shipping Forecast issued by the Meteorological Office at 0505 on Saturday, 9 November.
There are warnings of gales in all sea areas except Trafalgar.

The general synopsis at midnight. Low Malin 972 expected Sweden 966 by midnight tonight. Trough Malin to Shannon expected Fisher through Humber to Plymouth by same time.

29c The completed map for Example 1.

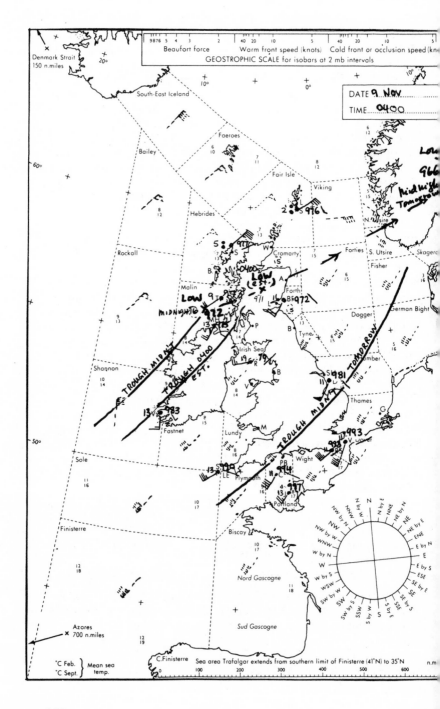

The area forecasts for the next 24 hours.

Viking E'ly backing NW'ly gale 8 to storm 10. Rain then showers. Moderate or poor becoming good.

North Utsire, South Utsire. SE becoming cyclonic then NW 7 to severe gale 9, decreasing 5 for a time. Occasional rain. Moderate or poor.

Forties. SW veering NW 7 to severe gale 9. Showers becoming wintry. Moderate or good.

Cromarty, Forth. Cyclonic 5 becoming NW'ly 6 to gale 8 increasing severe gale 9 in Cromarty later. Showers becoming wintry. Moderate or good.

Tyne, Dogger, Fisher, German Bight, Humber. SW veering NW 7 to severe gale 9. Squally showers. Good.

Thames, Dover, Wight, Portland, Plymouth, Biscay. SW veering W or NW 7 to severe gale 9 occasionally storm 10 in Biscay at first. Squally showers. Moderate or good.

Finisterre, Sole. SW veering N'ly gale 8 to storm 10, decreasing 6 to gale 8. Squally showers. Moderate or good.

Lundy, Fastnet, Irish Sea. SW veering N 6 to gale 8, occasionally severe gale 9 in Lundy and Fastnet at first. Showers. Moderate or good.

Shannon. N'ly gale 8 to storm 10. Rain then showers. Moderate or good.

Rockall, Malin, Hebrides. NE gale 8 to storm 10 occasionally violent storm 11 in Rockall and Hebrides, but cyclonic 6 in Malin at first. Rain then showers. Moderate becoming good.

Bailey, Fair Isle, Faeroes. NE backing NW severe gale 9 to violent storm 11, decreasing 6 to gale 8 in Bailey and Faeroes. Wintry showers. Moderate or good.

SE Iceland. NE backing N 7 to severe gale 9, decreasing 6. Wintry showers. Good. Light icing.

Coastal station reports for 0400 GMT.

Tiree. WSW 4. Recent rain. 9 miles. 973. Falling more slowly.

Butt of Lewis. NE 9. Continuous moderate rain. 5 miles. 977. Rising slowly.

Sumburgh. NE by E 7. Continuous moderate rain. 2 miles. 976. Falling more slowly.

Bell Rock. SW by S 4. 16 miles. 972. Falling.

Dowsing. SSW 10. 11 miles. 981. Falling.

Varne. SSW 9. 11 miles. 993. Rising slowly.

Royal Sovereign. SW by W 9. Recent showers. 11 miles. 993. Rising slowly.

30a Weather reports and major features (see Example 2).

Channel Light Vessel. SW 8. 11 miles. 994. Falling slowly.
Scilly. 0300 GMT. WSW 7. Recent showers. 13 miles. 990. Falling slowly.
Valentia. S by E 3. 13 miles. 983. Now rising.
Ronaldsway. W by S 5. 19 miles. 979. Rising.
Malin Head. SSW 5. 13 miles. 975. Falling more slowly.
Jersey. SW 5. 13 miles. 997. Now falling.

In the second case, for 9th November (Diagram 30a), assume that the forecast position 'Sweden' is as shown. The 0400 position may then be interpolated as 1/6 of 720 miles to give a position over the Grampians with a central pressure of 971 mb. In a similar fashion the position of the trough may be estimated as lying from Malin to SW Ireland. An examination of the winds, pressures and the estimated position of the low indicates a roughly circular pattern of winds (and therefore isobars) around a low centred over Scotland, but where should we begin with the isobars? The values from Sumburgh, Butt of Lewis, Tiree, Malin Head and Bell Rock are within 4 mb of 976, so begin with this isobar. The 984 line may be drawn from the Valentia and Dowsing observations, and the 992 using Scilly, Channel Light Vessel, Royal Sovereign and Varne pressures as a guide. These isobars are shown more boldly in Diagram 30b.

Now draw in the intermediate isobars over Britain packing them closer together where the winds are stronger (Dowsing) and farther apart where they are lighter (Ronaldsway). The chart shows that the low has already crossed over Scotland. This is commonly the case when a low is attempting to cross a mountainous region: the old low fills as it encounters the high ground and a new one forms on the 'lee' side of the barrier, an apparent leap-frog. In a similar manner a new trough of low pressure has formed over NE England in the lee of the Cumbrian mountains and the Pennines, tightening the pressure gradient over E and SE England (note 50 knots at Dowsing).

Now complete the isobar drawing over the sea areas by using the forecast winds and the Beaufort wind scale at the top of the chart. In this case a remnant of the old low may be drawn in Malin and the trough (a cold front) drawn from this centre to Valentia where the barometric tendency indicates that the trough has only just passed (now rising) though the wind has yet to veer (Diagram 30c). This cold front separates the 'southwesterlies' over the W parts of the British Isles from the northerlies to the W of Ireland. With such

30b **Beginning to add isobars.**

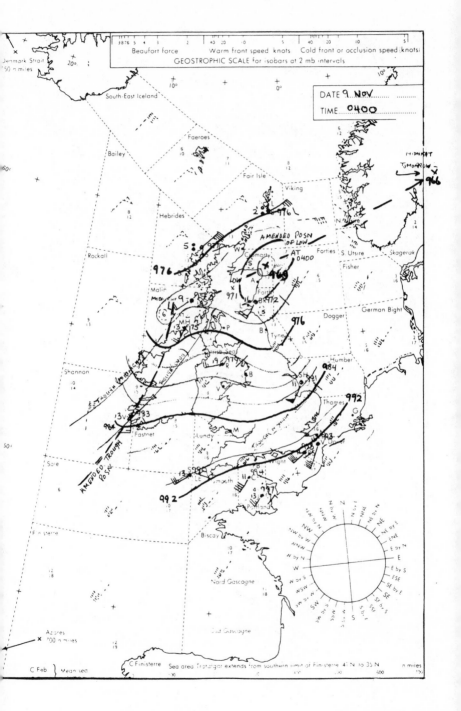

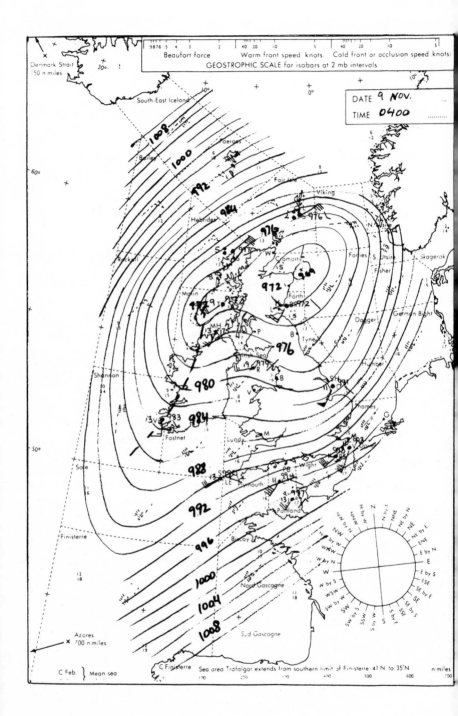

strong winds behind the cold front it is probable that the pressure trough would sharpen even further as it swung into S Britain, giving squally conditions as it passed by, which indeed was the case.

Example 3
The Shipping Forecast issued by the Meteorological Office at 1700 on Friday, 15 November.
There are warnings of gales in Viking, North Utsire, South Utsire, Forties, Cromarty, Forth, Trafalgar, Finisterre, Sole, Lundy, Fastnet, Irish Sea, Shannon, Rockall, Malin, Hebrides, Bailey, Fair Isle, Faeroes and SE Iceland.

The general synopsis at 1200. Low Humber 1022 moving slowly north and filling. Low 250 miles SW of Iceland 969 moving rather quickly N.

The area forecasts for the next 24 hours.
Viking, North Utsire, South Utsire, Forties, Cromarty, Forth. SE'ly 6 to gale 8 perhaps severe gale 9 later, but SW 4 at first in Cromarty and Forth. Rain at times. Moderate or good.
Tyne, Dogger. Cyclonic becoming SW'ly 5 to 7, perhaps gale 8 later. Occasional rain. Moderate or poor.
Fisher, German Bight. SE'ly 5 increasing 7, perhaps gale 8 later. Sleet at times. Moderate or poor.
Humber. Cyclonic becoming SW'ly 5 to 7, perhaps gale 8 later. Rain at time. Poor becoming moderate.
Thames, Dover. Mainly SW'ly 4 or 5 occasionally 6. Rain at first. Moderate.
Wight, Portland, Plymouth. Variable 3 becoming SW'ly 5 or 6. Rain later. Good becoming moderate or poor.
Biscay. Variable 3. Mainly fair. Good.
South Finisterre. NE'ly 4 or 5 occasionally 6 at first. Fair. Good.
North Finisterre. SW'ly 6 to gale 8 becoming variable 3. Occasional rain. Moderate or poor.
Sole, Lundy, Fastnet, Irish Sea. SW'ly 6 to gale 8 occasionally severe gale 9 in Sole at first, veering NW'ly 4. Occasional rain. Moderate or poor.
Shannon. S'ly gale 8 to storm 10, veering W'ly 6 to gale 8. Rain then showers. Moderate becoming good.
Rockall, Malin, Hebrides, Bailey. S or SE gale 8 to storm 10 occasionally violent storm 11 in Bailey, veering W or SW 6 to gale 8. Rain then showers. Moderate with fog patches, becoming good.

30c. **Completing the map for Example 2.**

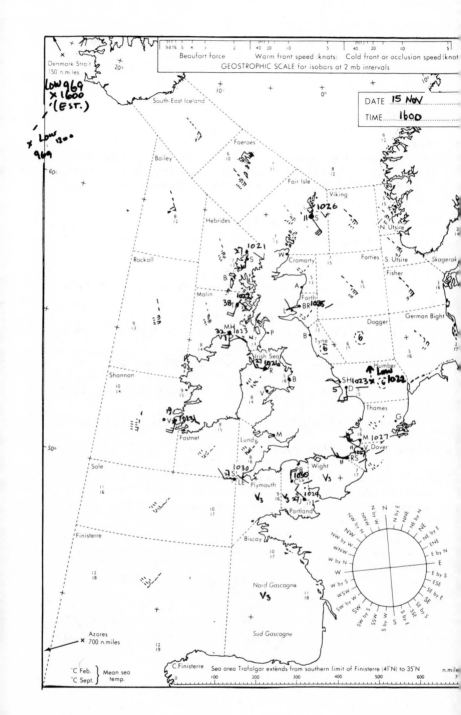

Fair Isle. SE'ly 7 to severe gale 9 veering NW'ly 6 to gale 8. Rain at times. Good becoming moderate.
Faeroes, SE Iceland. SE'ly gale 8 to storm 10 occasionally violent storm 11 in SE Iceland, veering W'ly 6 to gale 8. Rain then showers. Poor becoming good.

Coastal station reports for 1600 GMT.
Tiree. S by W 4. More than 38 miles. 1022. Falling.
Butt of Lewis. S 2. More than 27 miles. 1021. Falling.
Sumburgh. SE by S 6. 11 miles. 1026. Now rising.
Bell Rock. W by S 2. 16 miles. 1025. Rising slowly.
Dowsing. S 3. 5 miles. 1023. Steady.
Varne. WNW 4. 11 miles. 1027. Rising slowly.
Royal Sovereign. W 3. 11 miles. 1027. Rising slowly.
Channel Light Vessel. N 4. 11 miles. 1030. Steady.
Scilly. W 2. 27 miles. 1030. Falling slowly.
Valentia. S 5. Intermittent slight rain. 19 miles. 1023. Falling more slowly.
Ronaldsway. W 3. 27 miles. 1026. Falling more slowly.
Malin Head. S 4. 32 miles. 1023. Falling.
Jersey. NW 2. 27 miles. 1029. Rising slowly.

From the general synopsis for 15 November, the filling low may be estimated in N Humber at 1600 while the 'Iceland' low will be 120 miles N of the 'at first' position, i.e. 4 × 30 knots (the mean of the 'rather quickly' range of movement). The winds over most sea areas form the E and SE segments of the circulation around the deep low near Iceland, though this pattern is interrupted by a shallow low in Humber (Diagram 31a). The 1022 mb isobar over the western British Isles is a useful starting place. Then draw in the 1024 isobar over the W and N followed by the 1026 one. The latter will help with the drawing of a second 1024 isobar around the value 1023 at Dowsing. This will reposition the 'Humber' low. These initial isobars are drawn more boldly on Diagram 31b.

Now draw in the remaining isobars over Britain and complete the map by drawing to the forecast wind strengths over the sea areas (Diagram 31c). Incidentally, the 1030 isobar encloses a ridge of high pressure from the Azores to SW Britain.

A series of approximately six-hourly met maps will show the development of the synoptic features across the British Isles and NW Europe sea areas. It has already been said that almost all shipping forecasts are substantially correct: a very small number

31a   First plot, Example 3.

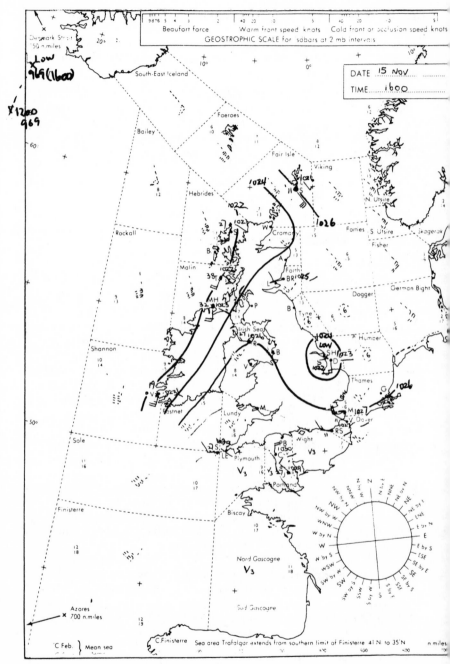

31b Constructing isobars.

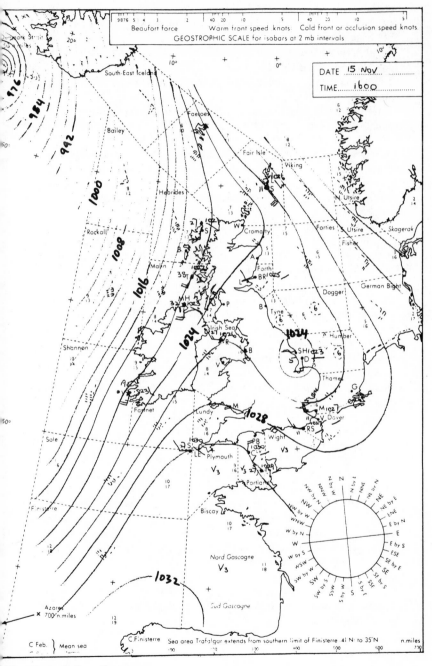

31b   Completing the map.

are, however, dramatically incorrect. In these circumstances a skipper may find himself off a dangerous lee shore. It is then no use blaming the forecast: he will have to get his craft out of this hazardous situation. By plotting a met-map and also keeping a weather eye lifted he will be able to detect that forecast developments may be incorrect, and will be much more able to make correct decisions.

Only a little practice will reduce the time required to produce a chart to a few minutes. This practice does not have to occur at sea; it can be carried out at any time. Having plotted a met-map from, say, the early morning forecast, watch the weather developments across your area during the day, noting the wind and sky changes as a low passes by. The next day's forecast will itself be a check on the accuracy of the synoptic predictions from the previous day's forecast.

On ocean passages, less detailed forecasts are available for most regions except parts of the Southern Ocean. These forecasts give the synoptic situation and its development over the next 24 hours over large ocean areas; some will also give wind forecasts. They are well worth listening to, especially in the temperate latitude belt, for they will reveal depression tracks at some distance so that the course may be adjusted to stay in favourable winds with good distances run rather than lying-to for possibly days at a time until headwinds and seas give way. The central areas of anticyclones may also be avoided in this fashion.

Some countries include a detailed analysis in code, giving the positions of highs and lows, of fronts, and of sufficient isobars to complete a chart. This broadcast is in Morse, but as the code used is in figures the task of taking this down is not as daunting as it would first appear, especially if a tape recorder is used. Again, an hour or so of effort here may save several days on total crossing time. The code is given in ALRS Vol 3. Those yachts equipped with Satfax (weather facsimile sets) will be able to receive analysis and forecast charts directly for the Atlantic at least up to several days ahead.

Within the tropics, where the main concern is tropical revolving storms such as hurricanes, there are numerous storm warning centres (Miami, Guam, Auckland, Darwin, Manila, Delhi et al) which issue detailed warnings. Since these are now based to a large extent on satellite surveillance, it is very unlikely that a storm will escape detection.

Full details of oceanic forecasts and tropical revolving storm warning centres are in ALRS Vol 3, and similar publications from other maritime nations.

THIRTEEN
Tropical Revolving Storms and Tactics for Avoiding Them

Hurricanes, typhoons and cyclones are the most destructive weather that one can meet at sea. Their effects over land and in relatively sheltered harbours are also potentially very dangerous. As the maps below show, they occur in some popular cruising regions. Only a very few yachts have – miraculously – survived mature storms at sea: it should be reckoned that small craft will founder in such conditions and therefore they must be avoided. Even large ships are sometimes lost.

The subject has been introduced in this book because it will affect the passage planning of some readers, especially those who intend to sail into tropical regions. The tactics for avoiding the worst effects of storms are also related to those for escaping less devastating gales. However, in a book of this length it cannot be covered fully, so readers with a particular interest are referred to my earlier book *Meteorology at Sea* where both theory and the seasonal and regional variations are discussed in more detail.

Tropical Revolving Storm is the name given to an often violent, cyclonic circulation of air which occurs within the tropics. It is similar in some ways to a depression of higher latitudes; the main differences are that its area is normally much smaller and, since the central pressures may be about the same as a depression, the pressure gradients are much steeper and therefore the winds are much stronger. They are classified according to the maximum wind speed near their centres: while winds remain at Force 7 or below, a Tropical Depression; maximum speeds between Force 8 and 9, a Moderate Tropical Storm; maximum between Forces 10 and 11, a Severe Tropical Storm; maximum Force 12 and above, a Hurricane (or other local name).

This is an almost internationally accepted classification, and the terms are used in radio warnings. In some areas different names are used; e.g. in the Indian Ocean sector, for the second and third stages 'Cyclonic' is substituted for 'Tropical'. The final mature stage is known as a Hurricane in the W Atlantic and E Pacific and in the SW Pacific, as a Typhoon in the W North Pacific, and as a Cyclone in the Indian Ocean.

Movement and Development

Hurricanes form over the warm tropical oceans and normally move westward at about 10 knots. Their development is due to the vast amount of latent heat which is released by vigorous convection within the associated cloud system and converted to a violent cyclonic wind system by the deflecting effect of the earth's rotation. The westward movement occurs on the Equatorward side of the sub-tropical high pressure belt. In summer and autumn (when hurricanes normally occur) the sub-tropical high pressure areas are confined to the oceans, so as the storms reach the western sides of the oceans they tend to be steered Poleward around the W side of the high-pressure region before moving away NE (or SE in the Southern Hemisphere) and then usually accelerating to about 20 knots. The typical path is a roughly parabolic curve; the 'elbow' is the 'point of recurvature'.

Some representative hurricane tracks for three of the regions are shown in Diagrams 32–34. These indicate the parabolic path sometimes followed, and also the high degree of variability of individual storm. It is this potential for changing course which is one of the main characteristics of tropical revolving storms. They must always be treated with caution, for even those which seem to be behaving in the 'typical' fashion may suddenly and dramatically turn through a right angle and charge away polewards. Some stop for a day or two before resuming the original track, while others

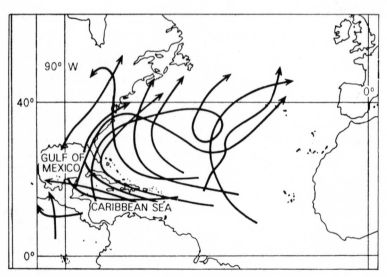

32   Typical hurricane tracks in the W North Atlantic.

perform a small loop or temporarily back-track before moving on.

Tropical revolving storms usually develop from 'disturbances' which are often no more than cloud clusters perhaps one or two hundred miles across. As they move westwards in the tropical latitudes, say 5°–15° N and S, some may take on a definite cyclonic circulation – the Tropical Depression stage – and of those some may become more vigorous – the Tropical Storm or Severe Tropical Storm stage. A few will develop into mature Hurricanes. The

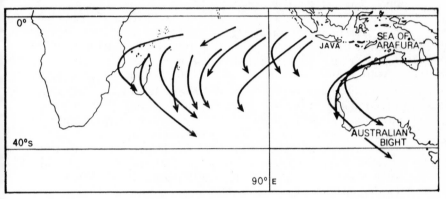

33   Cyclone tracks in the S Indian Ocean.

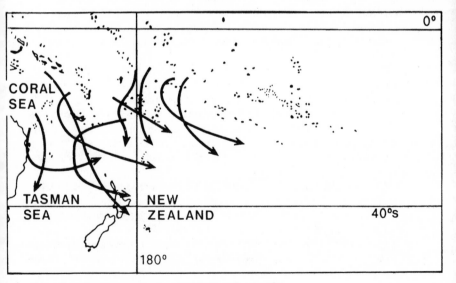

34   Hurricane tracks in the W South Pacific.

transition from cloud cluster to full hurricane may occur within only 24 hours.

The satellite picture of a mature hurricane shows some characteristic features. The main cloud mass may grow to about 500 miles across and into it several spiral feeder bands converge. At the centre of the cloud mass there is an almost cloud-free zone; this is the 'eye' and may be as much as 30 miles or so across. (Some satellite pictures have revealed a complex temporary double-eye structure, probably one vortex centre taking over from another within the small central section of the storm.) The clouds within the hurricane are thicker as the centre is approached. Rain becomes heavier until it is torrential within a ring of very thick cloud which itself contains the cloud-free eye of the hurricane; the inner edge of this annular cloud mass is called the Eye Wall.

Within the eye winds are light or calm though the sea is chaotic due to the huge waves entering the eye from practically every direction: any vessels are thrown around severely. Under the areas swept by the spiral feeder bands winds of at least Force 6 may be expected. Within the circular cloud mass Force 8 winds increase inwards, until normally at about 75 miles from the centre they will have risen to Force 12 or more (at least 64 knots). These are 'steady' or 'maximum sustained winds' and the gusts will be far stronger. The larger this circular mass, the stronger the winds. The strongest are found under the ring of thick cloud and torrential rain. Here, maximum sustained winds commonly exceed 100 knots in mature hurricanes. Steady speeds of over 130 knots have been estimated or recorded by aircraft; in the W North Pacific these have been designated Super-Typhoons. Similar super-storms probably occur in other regions.

Winds are anticlockwise in the Northern Hemisphere and clockwise in the Southern. The air drawn into a hurricane spirals inwards nearly horizontally at first, but with an increasing vertical component which reaches a maximum in the ring of cloud towards the centre. Within the eye the air is in fact slowly descending and hence almost cloud-free. Visibility within the inner regions of a hurricane apart from the eye is almost nil due to the constant heavy spray and torrential rain.

As long as a hurricane remains over a warm sea it normally retains its violence. Some do not recurve on reaching the western sides of the oceans but instead move over the continental land masses, where they usually die out in a day or two as their supply of moisture (latent heat) is cut off. As these storms approach the coast, sea levels rise far above normal and cause considerable flood damage, and there is real danger from flying debris. Currents produced as these boosted water levels build and recede are also

Satellite picture of a hurricane. (Photo courtesy NOAA)

phenomenal. These hazards are present even in so-called 'hurricane holes'.

After recurvature, those hurricanes which survive into the temperate latitudes are known as Extra-tropical Storms. Here their diameter has usually increased and their winds have decreased, though maximum sustained winds often still exceed Force 12. They often retain some semblance of an eye at this stage.

It is not unknown for such storms, having raged over the Caribbean and Gulf of Mexico, to have become extra-tropical and lashed the coasts of NW Europe with hurricane force winds a week or so later (Diagram 32). Similarly, typhoons have been known to survive a crossing of the whole North Pacific and to have caused considerable damage in British Columbia; while Coral Sea hurricanes have crossed the South Pacific to decay a week or so later around Cape Horn.

Regional Distribution and Seasons
In general the more mature tropical revolving storms occur over the central and western parts of the tropical oceans where the sea surface temperature is warmer than it is farther E. However, there are two areas of exception: on the E side of the North Pacific off the Central American coast, and off the W coast of Australia (Diagram 33). There sea temperatures in summer become high enough to generate tropical revolving storms. Another important exception is the absence of storms in the South Atlantic. The warm west-flowing South Equatorial Current is diverted by Brazil NW into the Caribbean so that the sea in the tropical South Atlantic is barely warm enough to develop these storms.

The main hurricane areas and the local names used are: the W North Atlantic including the Caribbean and Gulf of Mexico (Diagram 32); the E North Pacific; the W North Pacific (typhoons) including the South China Sea; the Arabian Sea and Bay of Bengal (cyclones); the South Indian Ocean (cyclones), (Diagram 33); the W South Pacific (Diagram 34).

Storm Surveillance and Warnings
Radio warning stations are listed in ALRS Vols 3 and 3a. Each area within the hurricane belt is covered by a responsible main met centre equipped to receive satellite pictures, both infra-red and visual so that day and night surveillance is maintained. Long-range radar and aircraft are also used.

It is fairly easy to detect tropical storms from satellite pictures as the area beyond the feeder bands is usually cloudless. A good estimate of the wind speeds can be made from the diameter of the circular cloud mass: the larger it is, the stronger the winds. It is unlikely that any storms will evade this intensive watch: indeed the statistics of frequency especially in such deserted areas as the

Indian Ocean will almost certainly be revised upwards when sufficient satellite data has been accumulated.

Storm warning centres must also predict path and speed over the next 24 hours or so. The warning will give the storm's position, its present strength amplified by estimates of its maximum sustained winds, and its predicted movement and development over the next 12 to 24 hours. These warnings will be repeated every few hours.

Since tropical revolving storms often behave in a most erratic manner, especially at recurvature, and since they may sometimes develop with explosive speed from cloud cluster to hurricane within 24 hours, it is obviously in a sailor's best interests to constantly monitor the storm's movement for himself from all visible signs as well as listening to all radio warnings.

Signs of Approach

Small vessels such as yachts should obviously avoid the hurricane season if possible. In the W North Pacific, typhoons may occur in any month. A listening watch should be kept for storm warnings and a weather eye kept lifted for the following signs of the approach or formation of a tropical revolving storm.

1. A long swell (crest-to-crest period over 10 seconds) is usually the first indication of a storm in the general area. The swell will be running out from the storm's centre.

2. A fall of pressure of about 3 mb below the values recorded at the same time over the past day or so. It is necessary to compare pressures for the same time of day on consecutive days because, especially in the tropics, there is a marked diurnal variation in pressure like an atmospheric tide. It is

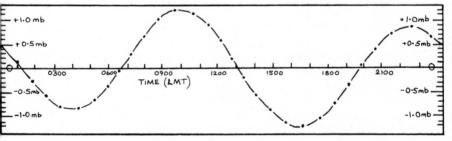

35   Diurnal variation of barometric pressure in the Tropics. The zero line is the average for the locality, given in Sailing Directions. If this is unknown, use the pressure recorded at the same time yesterday to determine the real change: if this is more than 3 mb, suspect that a tropical revolving storm is in the area.

characterized by peaks at 1000 and 2200 local time and troughs at 0400 and 1700, the range being 2 to 3 mb (Diagram 35).

3. Steadily thickening cloud, at first in the form of cirrus but later becoming darker and more threatening, especially if it is first observed in the direction of approach of the swell.

4. A freshening wind from a direction different from that which normally prevails over the area, such as the Trades or the Monsoons in the case of the South China Sea.

These four indicators, individually or particularly if occurring together, warn of the existence of a storm in the area. Spreading cloud and swell may give an indication of its bearing, otherwise it is difficult to determine its position and movement, but these must be known if any storm is to be avoided.

Avoiding Tropical Revolving Storms
The best indicator of the position and movement of a storm, other than radio warnings, is the wind itself. Having suspected the existence of a storm in the area, apply **Buys Ballots' Law**: back to the wind: low pressure is on your left (right) hand in the Northern (Southern) Hemisphere. In fact, while the wind remains no stronger than Force 6 the storm centre will lie about $70°$ on your left (right) hand, but when it reaches Force 8, now within the umbrella of the circular cloud mass and with the pressure about 5 mb lower than normal, the centre will draw farther aft to lie directly on your left (or right) hand in the Northern (or Southern) Hemisphere.

Bearings based on these assumptions, taken several hours apart, will give an indication of the storm's movement. Having determined this movement, avoiding action may be required. In this connection the terms Dangerous and Navigable Semicircles are often used, though the whole storm must be considered extremely dangerous to a yacht. These semicircles are separated by the storm's instantaneous track (Diagrams 36 and 37). To determine which semicircle one is in or about to enter, if the winds are such as to blow your craft into the projected track of the storm then she lies in the Dangerous Semicircle. If they will take her directly into the area just ahead of the storm she is in the Dangerous Quadrant. Conversely, if the winds are such as to blow her towards the rear of the storm, she is in the Navigable Semicircle.

Or in another form:
In the Northern Hemisphere, if the wind is veering the vessel must be in the Dangerous Semicircle; and if backing she is in the Navigable Semicircle.

In the Southern Hemisphere, if the wind is backing, the vessel must be in the Dangerous Semicircle; and if veering she is in the Navigable Semicircle.

These rules always apply in both Hemispheres irrespective of the storm's movement.

It is important to remember that these storms sometimes back-track, albeit infrequently, so that almost without warning the Navigable Semicircle becomes the Dangerous one and vice versa.

Diagrams 36 and 37 are schematic representations of the wind field around a hurricane in the Northern and Southern Hemispheres. Craft seriously threatened by a hurricane may be in any of three positions relative to it: dead ahead of the storm track,

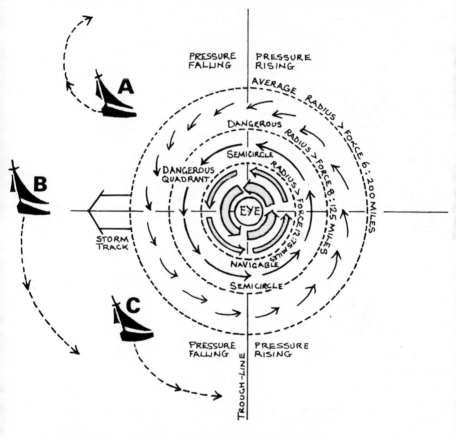

36 Tactics for avoiding a hurricane in the Northern Hemisphere (see text also).

or in either the Dangerous or Navigable Semicircle. Having determined which, the following action should be taken immediately. The letters A, B, C refer to the respective Diagrams.

Northern Hemisphere   Diagram 36

A. A sailing yacht in or about to enter the Dangerous Semicircle (wind veering) should broad-reach on starboard tack and maintain that point of sailing by progressively altering course to starboard as the wind veers until the pressure begins to rise, by which time the storm will move away (see trough line).

B. A yacht dead ahead of the storm should maintain a broad reach on starboard tack by progressively altering course to port as the wind backs, until the pressure begins to rise.

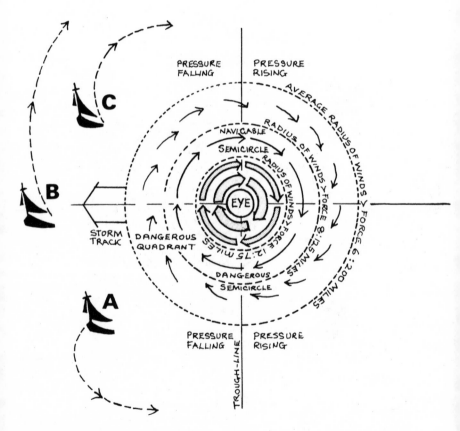

37   Tactics for avoiding a hurricane in the Southern Hemisphere (see text also).

C. A yacht in or about to enter the Navigable Semicircle should also maintain a broad reach on starboard tack by progressively altering to port as the wind backs, until the pressure begins to rise.

Southern Hemisphere   *Diagram 37*
A. A sailing yacht in or about to enter the Dangerous Semicircle (wind backing) should broad-reach on port tack and maintain that point of sailing by progressively altering course to port as the wind backs.
B. A yacht dead ahead of the storm should maintain a broad reach on port tack by altering to starboard as the wind veers.
C. A yacht in or about to enter the Navigable Semicircle should also maintain a broad reach on port tack by altering to starboard as the wind veers.

To summarize the rules for detection and avoidance of tropical revolving storms:
Detection: from barometric pressure, swell, wind from unusual direction, high cloud increasing and thickening.
Position and Movement: apply Buys Ballot's Law to determine the storm's bearing. A second bearing later should show the storm's track.
Avoidance: in the Northern Hemisphere: put the wind on your starboard quarter and keep it there. In the *Southern Hemisphere* put the wind on your port quarter and keep it there.

But better still avoid the hurricane season, and if this is not possible then keep a continual listening watch for radio storm warnings.

Tropical storms are given names. In the western North Pacific the names of typhoons run alphabetically irrespective of calendar, but in most other sectors the names restart with A each season. In the North Atlantic the name of any storm which has caused considerable damage is never reused for another.

INDEX

METEOROLOGY AT SEA

Ray Sanderson

A more extensive treatment of this subject, with greater emphasis on met theory. The section on wind and weather patterns on Transatlantic routes, and in the Baltic, Med, Pacific and Australia are invaluable for cruise planning.

The author is a Forecaster at the Bracknell Meteorological Office and is also an experienced seaman.

Contents include:
– Factors producing winds, precipitation, altered visibility, fog.

– Pressure features and the movement of weather systems in both Northern and Southern Hemispheres.

– Signs of approaching bad weather.

– The use of forecasts and weather maps. Foreign sea forecast areas.

– Hurricanes, typhoons and cyclones: movement, signs of approach and avoidance tactics.

– Weather in the main Atlantic and Pacific sea areas, the Baltic and Mediterranean, and around the British Isles.

For a complete free catalogue of nautical books, write to Stanford Maritime Ltd, 12 Long Acre, London WC2E 9LP, U.K.

227 pages   Extensively illustrated with cloud photos and 170 diagrams and maps

ISBN 0 540 07405 5

STANFORD MARITIME

259
207
306